Invisible Ink

Invisible Ink

A Family Memoir

MARTHA LEIGH

Matador
9 Priory Business Park,
Wistow Road, Kibworth Beauchamp,
Leicestershire. LE8 0RX
Tel: 0116 279 2299
Email: books@troubador.co.uk
Web: www.troubador.co.uk/matador
Twitter: @matadorbooks

ISBN 978 180046 038 6
EBOOK ISBN 978 1800467 620
AUDIOBOOK ISBN 978 1800467 736

British Library Cataloguing in Publication Data.
A catalogue record for this book is available from the British Library.

Printed and bound by CPI Group (UK) Ltd, Croydon, CR0 4YY
Typeset in 11pt Minion Pro by Troubador Publishing Ltd, Leicester, UK

Matador is an imprint of Troubador Publishing Ltd

To Huw with all my love.

You never met my parents but now you know them well.

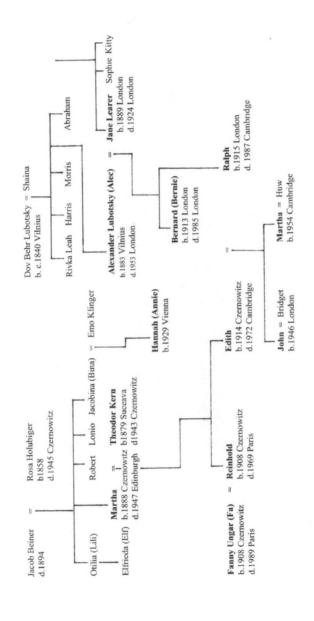

Simplified Family Tree

CONTENTS

FOREWORD

This family memoir has been waiting to be written for several decades. Ever since my childhood, I had known about the boxes that were stuffed in various cupboards around the house containing my parents' correspondence. This began in 1937 when they met in Paris and continued throughout the six years of the war. Writing to each other sometimes in German, but mostly in French, their peculiar love story evolved with hiccups and tension against the turbulent background of their lives and world events.

Later, more letters emerged from the loft of the house I grew up in. These were from my mother's mother in Czernowitz, a remote town in eastern Europe. I had to wait much longer before discovering their contents because they were written in Sütterlin, a German handwriting script which was totally illegible to me. Eventually I found a native German speaker who could decipher it, which brought my warm, witty and lovable grandmother to life.

My father left an extensive personal archive. Very helpfully, he kept both the letters he received and drafts of his own, taking care to date them. After his death, much more of his personal writing came to light: this included poems composed from the age of fifteen to the year of his death, a play, his eye-witness account of the Battle of Cable Street in 1936, some short stories, diaries, notebooks of quotations and aphorisms, intimate correspondence with friends, some very moving letters he wrote to his mother when he was nine years old and an astonishingly frank novel.

My mother, a concert pianist, expressed her deepest feelings through music. In her letters, as in her life, she tended to be economical with the truth, but those who loved her could tell when she was holding back. Her letters to my father give an outline of her traumatic war experiences, and the Swiss Federal Archives have filled in some of the gaps. When on twice-weekly dialysis, realising she was dying, she set about in a purposeful way to give me an account of what she had endured during the war. Each time I visited, there was a new instalment. Alas, at the age of seventeen I did not retain everything she told me. I only wish she had committed her story to paper.

My mother's brother, my Uncle Reinhold, was nothing less than a modern hero. A man of action and a scientist, he wrote a memoir called *Mes quatre vies* which he tape-recorded when he was ill, continuing until a few days before his death. This has been a very useful source of information. In it he relates his extraordinary exploits during the war in France, and his rise from working as a country doctor to his position as the nation's leading anaesthetist. His cousin, Annie, whom he adopted, has also written two memoirs which relate her miraculous escapes from the Nazis.

All these documents demanded to be read in the first place so that I could satisfy my personal curiosity, uncover secrets, find out who my parents really were and by extension, understand my own identity. This turned into a much wider exploration. The family history is entwined with many of the social and political currents in Europe during the twentieth century. The letters also provide a close-up view of daily life in that era which seems so long ago, when seen from a twenty-first century perspective.

I agonised about whether I should publish information my father had kept private during his lifetime. I concluded that, as a seeker of truth himself, he would approve. After all, had he not dedicated a lifetime to researching every detail about that flawed genius, Jean-Jacques Rousseau, himself the author of *The Confessions*? He expressed a longing for a world in which he would be understood, and there are clues that he had an eye to posterity. For a long time, he had intended to publish his novel. He could easily have destroyed his writing. Instead he preserved it with the meticulous attention of a true archivist.

My father must have enjoyed the prospect of his children sorting through his personal documents. With his characteristic wicked humour, he left us a sheet of paper, blank apart from the heading, "This page is written in invisible ink."

1

PORSON ROAD

I was born in 1954, just nine years after the Second World War, but it could have been ninety as far as I was concerned.

We moved into a brand-new house, Number 12 Porson Road, when I was four. It was about two miles south of Cambridge city centre on the way to Trumpington. The house was the product of my father's dreams and the answer to my mother's prayers. My father, Ralph Alexander Leigh, had bought the plot which had once been farmland and was still full of turnips. When we first moved in, pigs roamed in the garden and occasionally cows appeared from the neighbouring field, which was a mass of buttercups in spring. Ours was the last to be built during my childhood, in the road of large detached residences with orderly gardens.

Ralph himself, with the help of an architect, designed the house from scratch, which accounted for several eccentricities: the most puzzling of these, persisting in my memories and my dreams throughout my life, was the absurd arrangement of the front and back door being next to each other. The front door was sturdy and secure. It opened onto a spacious hallway with an impressive parquet floor and a very high ceiling from which hung a dusty chandelier full of cobwebs, a wedding present from my Uncle

Bernie. The back door was reached from inside, through a small washroom and lavatory with turquoise vinyl tile flooring. It did not lock properly, and this was never fixed. Consequently, despite its rather imposing main entrance, the house never felt quite secure.

For Ralph, the house was an expression of elegance and grandeur. The expansive drawing room could accommodate both my mother's grand pianos but was usually reserved for the best one (which she referred to as 'a superior instrument'). It occupied one corner of the parquet floor which emerged from underneath a huge Turkey carpet. Above the splendid, grey marble fireplace hung a painting, which my father believed to be valuable, showing a ship coming into harbour – you could just make it out under the varnish. In the alcoves on either side of the fireplace, he displayed his collection of Imari vases and plates and his blue glass vases and bowls. The drawing-room doors were eighteenth century in style, with gold-painted mouldings in the panels and crystal knobs. There was an overloaded, precariously tilting, revolving bookcase and a huge glass-fronted cabinet in which my mother kept her music and my father his liqueurs and cut-glass decanters filled with sherry, both sweet and dry, to accompany the salted roasted peanuts and pimento-stuffed olives he offered to visitors. The French windows overlooking the garden on two sides of the room made it very bright, causing the dusky red damask curtains and upholstery to fade.

The garden was my father's territory. He adored it and it gave him joy to inspect it with me every day in spring and summer. Beyond the vast lawn and borders was a large orchard with many varieties of apples, pears, currant bushes and soft fruits. We delighted in picking the asparagus which came up every day when it was in season. Many of the plants Ralph had chosen were inspired by his happy stay before the war in the Loire Valley, where he tutored the sons of a French family: espalier fruit trees, *Doyenne du Comice* pears, a yellow climbing rose called

'Madame de something or other', Mirabelle cherry plums... My mother got into trouble for cooking the strawberries. My father and I made quince and crab apple jelly in the autumn, turning the kitchen into a sticky mess.

My mother, Edith Helen Leigh, née Kern, took virtually no interest in the garden, hardly ever setting foot in it. The exception to this was the hedge of Queen Elizabeth roses (a very modern rose, bred to celebrate the coronation) which formed the boundary of our front garden. As soon as she caught sight of the familiar pink blooms as she approached from a distance, Edith would feel she was returning to a safe haven.

Edith referred to herself as a 'B.F.' which stood for 'bloody foreigner'. Although she had become completely fluent in English and read avidly in the language, she never lost her Central European accent. She often referred to the situation ironically: there was the story of her going to buy shoes; the assistant, a young man, gave up trying to find a suitable pair to fit her broad feet, saying with a sigh, "I'm afraid, Madam, you have continental feet!" Whenever she was footsore and weary, she complained that she was suffering from continental feet. She made the decision not to speak German, even to her cousin. Sadly, this prevented me from becoming bilingual, since she barely taught me any of that language apart from a string of endearments and nicknames which she could not restrain: 'Puppele, Puperl, Katzi, Schatzi, Hasili, Spatzi, Mäderl'. She and my father still spoke French occasionally, especially if they did not want me or my brother to understand. I quickly picked up the meaning of pas devant les enfants. My mother sometimes asked my father for a baiser d'encouragement when faced with an unpleasant or daunting chore, and she often referred with irony to Ralph's intelligence supérieure when asking him to do something for her that required male strength.

Edith loved the house. At certain times, such as when she was dealing with the laundry in the linen cupboard, she seemed to communicate her contentment wordlessly. She projected special status onto certain places in the house: 'the red table', 'the cats' bedroom' (where the cats slept when they were ill), 'the fish', meaning the large black and yellow fish-shaped mat in the bathroom, 'the little study' where she taught and practised the piano.

If I had to think of one word to describe my childhood, I would say that it was quiet. The house contained the separate worlds of its inhabitants. My brother John, who was eight years older than me, spent much of his time as a day boarder at the Leys School for Boys, and when he came home, generally led his own life. During the day at weekends or after school, I played with several children in the road whose parents were also academics. Stephen's father next door was a research chemist, as was Elizabeth's, who was known as 'F.G.' Most intriguing was Vivienne's father, who was researching into the 'primordial soup'.

My father, a Fellow of Trinity, spent a part of every day involved in his other life at College. When at home, he would be in his study at his enormous antique desk, originally a lacemaker's table. Surrounded from floor to ceiling by his collection of eighteenth-century books, he hammered at speed on his typewriter, editing the *Complete Correspondence of Jean-Jacques Rousseau* in forty-nine volumes. I used to love to sit beneath the desk, listening to the regular 'ting, ting' as he reached the end of a line. Pretending to be a cat, I tried to sneak in unnoticed, but he would soon say, "I know you're there." Sometimes he shared some sweets he had bought at the market wrapped in a triangular paper bag with twirled ends. He usually carried on working into the small hours. Although we all lived with 'poor Jean-Jacques', as my father called him, or perhaps it is truer to say that Jean-Jacques lived with us, I could not say I became very knowledgeable about him, much beyond knowing what year in the eighteenth century we had reached – the years crawled towards the French Revolution in my father's study.

Paradoxically, perhaps, what my parents had most in common was solitude. My mother practised the piano for eight hours a day whenever she could – that is whenever she was not teaching. She believed in what she called 'botty patience'. I heard her pieces so often that I was able to sing all the melodies from her extensive repertoire. Her 'little study' was downstairs, immediately beneath my bedroom. Sometimes, when I was a teenager and was finding it difficult to get up in the morning, she would play me my favourite pieces to encourage me to bestir myself. I remember particularly a Chopin study in A flat major. She could be irate if the phone interrupted her practice and was known to answer in a fit of fury, "There's no-one in!" slamming down the receiver.

There was little overlap between all our worlds: occasionally my father came home late in the evening, slightly merry, with a small group of male friends from College whom he called 'the wee folk' on account of him being so tall and they a lot shorter. He would cook scrambled eggs for them while they put the record player on at high volume (I remember lying in bed hearing blasts from *Carmina Burana*). Fellows of the College and their families were invited to the Christmas party at the Master's Lodge, a grand affair with an enormous glittering tree. It was a little daunting, as a small child, climbing up the huge staircase to be greeted by Lord and Lady Butler at the top. The first time, I was unprepared for shaking 'Rab' Butler's withered hand. Once inside, I loved to see the huge, full-length portrait of Queen Elizabeth I in her bejewelled dress, orange wig and enormous white ruff resembling a mass of snowflakes. Ralph also took his brother, Bernie, to the College Christmas Feast, and once when Bernie stayed the night in College, he claimed he had slept in the same room as Queen Victoria.

Uncle Bernie was a constant presence in my childhood. He came to stay with us in Porson Road every other weekend. He was as generous, loving and good-natured an uncle as one could possibly have. Although, superficially, he and Edith did not have much in common, they got on very well. One of the things they shared (apart from their adulation of Ralph) was their monastic lifestyle. Neither of them had any material wants or needs and Bernie helped Edith with day to day chores such as the grocery shopping. Ralph did not concern himself with such matters and tried to avoid Uncle Bernie and his 'stinking pipe'.

I do not recall my parents sharing many interests. They were both so absorbed in their own vocation that they did not spend much time doing things with me either. Family activities with both my parents were so infrequent that they stand out in my mind, mostly as times of great happiness: watching all twenty-six episodes of *The Forsyte Saga* on television together, having tea on a hot summer's day on the Bowling Green of Trinity College; the tea had a dash of smoky China in it, the tomato sandwiches were delicious despite being warm and a bit soggy, and the rich fruit cake was the best I have ever tasted.

Although we did not do much together as a family, I was close to both my parents in different ways. My most intimate times with my father took place when he was getting washed and dressed to go out and when we had tea together. He would often return from College at around 4pm, just after I had returned from school. On his way home, he was fond of visiting the market, where he would scour the stalls for any bargains and the cheapest oranges. The front door would slam shut with its characteristic reassuring and resounding crunch, and we would sit at the red Formica kitchen table together over tea and biscuits – Rich Tea, or Garibaldi (squashed flies), Ginger Nuts, or Jaffa Cakes and sometimes cake. Ralph had a weakness for the gaudy pink and yellow Battenburg. He was obliged to cut down on all of this in the sixties when he grew fat for the first time in his life, developing diabetes. Conversation was wide-ranging – politics, current affairs, social injustice, literature, art and music, and he would also often ruminate on his friendships and personal relationships. I was content to be a sounding board. I sometimes wondered if he had another family elsewhere. What my mother was doing during these tea-time chats I am not sure. She could have been teaching or practising in the 'little study' or maybe she was in London.

My father loved my company when he was preparing to go out. There were no inhibitions from his side about nudity, which I suppose was helpful for a girl attending a single-sex school, but inappropriate by the time I reached puberty. He would often hum or sing favourite arias from Mozart operas whilst washing and shaving, and afterwards apply talcum powder and liberal splashes of perfume. My mother regularly received toiletries for Christmas from one of her pupils who worked for Helena Rubinstein. She tried to save them in the bottom of her chest of drawers to give away later as presents, but they were eagerly intercepted by Ralph; his favourite brand was *Emotion*. When getting ready to go out, he liked to consult me when choosing a silk tie from his vast collection. His best shirts were embroidered for him by his devoted cousin, Rose, with his initials 'R.A.L.' in red silk, just below the breast pocket, where he would place a crisply ironed, carefully folded handkerchief.

My mother, on the other hand, was so modest that I never saw her naked all at once – only one half at a time on separate occasions. Her approach to clothes was purely pragmatic: what would last, was the best value and would be most flattering by hiding the bulges. The solution was usually a donkey-brown or navy-blue suit with three-quarter-length sleeves. Aunt Fa, Edith's bossy sister-in-law from Paris, was never satisfied with my mother's outfits. One year she proclaimed, "Edith, you absolutely must shorten your hemline, it's much too long" and the following year, needless to say, it was 'much too short'. Edith also had a collection of hats which she wore well into the sixties. She was very annoyed with my brother and me when we ruined two of them which we had stolen to wear whilst painting a ceiling.

She had two full-length concert dresses, one of dark grey silk covered with fluttering lighter grey organza with black spots, the other of dark red silk with a fine, black reticular material flowing over it, which she wore with a pair of elegant black suede heels. Before giving a concert, she could transform herself into a beauty, with her blonde hair freshly permed, a dash of powder and some lipstick. For many years after she died, I was unable to part with her concert shoes (despite being incapable of walking in them). I also kept her well-worn, dowdy, brown suede, furry, zip-up bootees.

Edith had limited connections or interest in life beyond the house and her inner world of music. In fact, she made no new English friendships in Cambridge and was generally rather uneasy with social contact. She was certainly in awe of Mrs Smith next door and made strenuous efforts not to put a foot wrong. "What will Mrs Smith say?" was her reaction to my sunbathing in my swimsuit in the garden. She viewed the neighbours, several of whom were full-time mothers, with some incomprehension, but was always at pains to make sure I was on my best behaviour whenever I went to play with their children in their houses. Similarly, she was not relaxed when I brought school friends to the house, although she tried to make them welcome. If term had started, she would ask, "Are you looking forward to the holidays?" and if it was school holiday time, "Are you looking forward to going back to school?" Many a time she told me that she 'wanted me to have a happy childhood' and that she was sure that I wouldn't want her to be 'just a housewife'. She planned my summer holidays so that I was entertained, which usually involved paying somebody else to look after me.

Her lack of confidence in the outside world was no doubt exacerbated by her very poor eyesight. Holding her hand when crossing the road did not feel safe. This has left both my brother and me with a lifelong fear of traffic. Her vision was so bad that when we were waiting for the bus, she would say hopefully, "I think I can see something red coming," which was not necessarily a bus. Walking with my father was quite different. I was happy to put my hand in his which was large and warm, although it was difficult keeping up with the stride of a man of six foot three inches. Unlike nearly all the other families in our road, we did not have a car since neither of my parents could drive. Ralph was reluctant to try it again after driving a lorry into a ditch when he was in the army, and Edith was too impractical and too short-sighted.

Edith's philosophy, which she drummed into me from an early age, was that of 'fitting in'. The matter of religion sticks in my mind in this regard. While I was growing up, I had no sense of the family belonging to any faith (apart from sporadic attempts by Uncle Bernie to educate me in matters Jewish). When we moved to Neuchâtel in Switzerland in 1959 for a year, so that my father could pursue his research on Jean-Jacques Rousseau, my mother told me that I must tell the teacher that I was Catholic. Once back again in England, I assumed that I was Catholic, but that was wrong according to her. I was Protestant. She was a great believer in 'white lies' especially if it was 'all for your own good'. One day Tigger, whom I loved passionately, (he was one of a succession of cats with the same name) disappeared from the house after a period of illness. My mother explained that Tigger had gone to a farm to benefit from the fresh air. At the age of seven, I made a pretence of believing her.

My father went away about three times a year to use the libraries in Paris and Neuchâtel for his research. When I was a small child, I remember that my mother arranged that I should sleep with her in the parental double bed while Ralph was away. She said that she thought it would be nice for us both. The first time I was woken up by her strangulated scream in the middle of the night I was terrified. She always longed for my father to return and we would sit on the stairs together by the window watching out for him to appear. She would say that, even after so many years of marriage, her heart would beat faster when she heard his footstep.

Edith also left the house regularly. On Wednesdays and Thursdays every week during term-time she would be in London, teaching the piano at the French Lycée in South Kensington (or 'Sowss Kensington' as she pronounced it). Although she often declared, "I feel as much like going to Sowss Kensington as flying to the moon," she probably did enjoy this opportunity to meet her cousin, Elf (Elfrieda), who was more like a sister to her, and perhaps Erica, an old childhood friend. They could go and have a boiled egg or a sausage at a Lyons' Corner House and then go on to the cinema.

At home, Ralph would be cooking for me and trying to convince me that 'Daddy's stew' or soused mackerel were delicacies. He always thought his cooking was superior to Edith's and never let her forget that she had once boiled an avocado which she had bought as an experiment. Although she did have a repertoire of Austro-Hungarian dishes (when I was small I did not understand the meaning of *Zwetschken Knödel mit Butter Soss* – plum dumplings with butter sauce – but I loved the sound of it), we ate a lot of convenience foods: fish fingers, baked beans, Knorr soups (especially Spring Vegetable and Oxtail), frankfurters and ready-made fruit tarts. I noticed, however, that our eating habits were not the same as those of my school friends. My parents knew all about yoghurt (which they pronounced 'yeoguourt') and we could not eat salad without a vinaigrette. None of the children I played with had pickled cucumbers as a staple in their larder. What other father waited for the top of the milk to go sour and then made a dish called *smetana* out of it with spring onions and radishes? These and other small differences made me feel it was difficult to 'fit in' and appear thoroughly British with my friends. In those times it was unusual not to be so and I always felt different.

On Fridays, my mother sometimes made a special meal for me, such as steak and chips, or *Wienerschnitzel* which she bashed with a wooden mallet to make it thin and tender. As a real treat and at great expense, she served me a whole wineglassful of orange juice from a tin. Unfortunately, she set fire to the plastic kitchen curtains (with their motif of teapots and kettles) more than once when frying chips. At weekends she cooked English breakfast for my father and brother (including kippers on special occasions) whilst my father disappeared behind *The Times*, wearing his stripy dressing gown which was too short.

To all intents and purposes, Edith was indifferent to the material world. She never asked for anything for herself or seemed to want anything. This made it very difficult to buy her a present for Christmas or her birthday. If I asked her what she wanted, she might answer after racking her brains, "Well, perhaps you could buy me a pencil, or a rubber, maybe."

Nobody enjoyed Christmas in my family. By coincidence, both my grandmothers had died on Christmas Eve, long before I was born. Granny Martha, my mother's mother, collapsed and died on the way to the cinema. My father's story was that his 'poor Mummy' (Granny Jane) died of pneumonia at the age of thirty-five when he was only nine years old. This must have contributed to the tensions in the family at Christmas; Ralph was always in a filthy mood when he tried to set up the lights on the Christmas tree which inevitably failed to work – leading to a sense of humour failure, never mind the lights. Sadly, I do not remember anything in the house that had come from my grandmother, Jane. Ralph spent years searching for the dinner service he remembered from his childhood. It was white with a floral pattern in a sea-green colour. Over the years he built up quite a collection of near matches but never found the real thing. It was only when he was about sixty, when Uncle Bernie suddenly remembered that he had had their mother's crockery all along in his flat. Ralph was overjoyed when Bernie gave it to him. At last he had his mother's tureens, platters, jugs and dishes.

Sometimes my father was very irritable and apt to explode. Edith always tried to soothe and calm her 'Ralphie' down, warning us not to 'go near the lion's den' because he was 'very nervy today'. Everybody around him would try to make allowances, myself included. As Uncle Bernie said, "You must understand that Ralph is very brilliant, but he is under a lot of strain. He's very sensitive." My mother only expressed anger non-verbally, usually with what she called a *Basiliskenblick* – a basilisk's stare.

When my brother, John, was at home, he tried to teach me some basics about cricket in the garden. We also had a passion for a game called 'clock golf' which involved laying down a circular golf course with twelve holes in the lawn and hitting a ball into the holes. By winter the holes had subsided and were covered with grass. In our family, when something was broken, there was no thought of salvaging or mending it, since no-one had the time or skills: it was simply replaced. And so it was that eventually there were at least three generations of clock golf buried under the lawn. When I looked out of my window to the over-familiar garden that I loved so well, where I knew every flower and every tree, there was no longer any hint or sign of it. In our quiet, suburban existence, a little more than a decade after the Second World War, there was so much more going on under the surface which I sensed during my childhood but could not articulate.

2

CZERNOWITZ

When I was growing up, my notion of where my mother came from was very confused. She gave me various descriptions of the location of her home town, Czernowitz: sometimes she said vaguely that it was in Central Europe, or that it was near Moldova or Bessarabia which sounded exotic, or that it was part of a region called Bukovina which I discovered means 'Land of the beech trees'. Most often she referred to it as part of Austria, informing me that I was 'half Austrian'. For me, Czernowitz belonged to a far-off legendary land, a place my mother had left when she was seventeen, never to return. In fact, throughout my childhood and youth, Czernowitz was in the Soviet Union behind the Iron Curtain. It was effectively inaccessible until after the fall of communism, and therefore a place I never expected to be able to see for myself. Since all discussions about Czernowitz inevitably begin with a long preamble about its remoteness, its elusiveness and complex political history, which most books clarify with a map, here is one now.

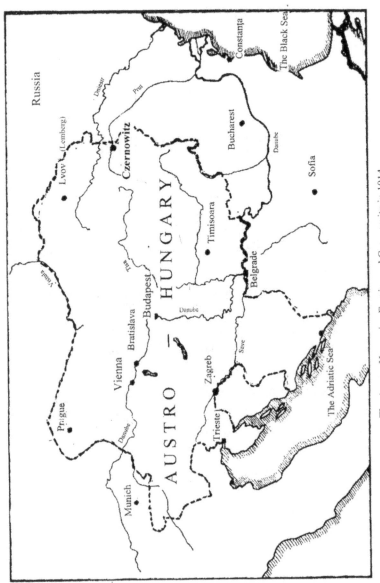

The Austro-Hungarian Empire and Czernowitz in 1914

Today Czernowitz belongs to Ukraine and is called 'Chernivtsi' (*Чернівці*). My mother's family, however, was neither Ukrainian nor Russian. They considered themselves Austrian, and the fact that they were Jewish was of no importance to them. When my mother was born, Czernowitz was still the farthest eastern outpost of the Austro-Hungarian Empire. The Russians invaded the town at the onset of the First World War, after which it became part of Romania until 1940. The possession of the city chopped and changed during the Second World War: in 1940 it was briefly occupied by the Russians for a year followed by the Nazis (assisted by the Romanians) who were finally defeated by the Soviets in 1944. Thereafter it belonged to the Soviet Union until 1991, when Ukraine became independent.

The political vicissitudes were to inflict suffering on the Jewish citizens of Czernowitz, including my family, that they could never have imagined. After the Second World War, most of those who had not been exterminated fled. Considering the extraordinary political upheavals of the twentieth century, Czernowitz today is surprisingly well preserved in terms of bricks and mortar. However, an entire population with all its culture has been swept away.

In retrospect, the last decades of the nineteenth century and the early years of the twentieth century represented a golden epoch, an all too fleeting period of stability. My mother's mother's side of the family, the Beiners, had flourished in Czernowitz for generations. The Austrian Emperor, Joseph II, passed the Edict of Jewish Tolerance in 1782, which accorded equal rights to Jews, protecting them from persecution. Oppressed Jews, fleeing from pogroms in Poland, Russia and neighbouring Galicia, were drawn to settle in Czernowitz.

It is more likely, however, that the Beiners came to Czernowitz in the early nineteenth century from further west where German was spoken. One of Joseph II's successors was

Kaiser Franz Joseph, who ruled from 1848 to 1916. A well-loved legend exists to account for further liberal measures taken by him with respect to the Jews of Czernowitz: in 1880 he went on a tour of Moravia, Galicia and Hungary, visiting Czernowitz on the way. After crossing the bridge on the River Prut, he was obliged to go through the poorest Jewish quarter in the city. Exhausted, he decided to stop at the nearest inn, where some poor Jews received him and served him refreshments – pickled herring, bread and garlic. Unfortunately, a herring bone stuck in his throat and he started to choke. One of the men tried thumping the Kaiser on the back as he went red and then blue. The situation was becoming desperate and it looked as though he was about to asphyxiate. What to do? Panicking, they fetched the woman of the house from the kitchen. She rapidly appraised the situation, asked the Kaiser to open his mouth wide, and then, heavily exhaling garlicky breath over him, proceeded to remove the fish bone from his throat with her grubby hands and dirty fingernails. Overcome with gratitude, the Kaiser asked her to let him grant her a wish. She replied that she had no wish: life as a Jew was so miserable that she would be better off dead. But the men who were in the room were quick to ask the Kaiser to improve the lot of the Jews, to which he readily agreed, granting further freedoms. Unlike their counterparts in the rest of central Europe they now had permission to own property, move freely, join any profession and enter the sphere of politics.

In 1875, a new university opened in Czernowitz, in a very fine building, formerly a bishop's palace. This attracted a further wave of people to the town, one of whom was my grandfather, Theodor Kern. His father was a self-made businessman who lived in Burdujeni, a small town in southern Bukovina near Suceava, part of the principality of Moldova at that time, and now in Romania. A practising Jew running a successful enterprise (there are no family records to say what this was) but with little formal education himself, my great-grandfather was able to send his son, Theodor, to the splendid new university in Czernowitz. Later he lost all his money, presumably in the Great Crash of 1929.

The extended family was scattered throughout the Austro-Hungarian Empire – some relatives living in Austria itself and some in Hungary, as well as all those in Czernowitz. Edith's mother, my grandmother, Martha, refers to travelling freely within the Empire to visit family. Vienna was about eighteen hours away from Czernowitz by the night train. The unique relationship between Czernowitz and Vienna goes back to 1774 when Austria won Czernowitz from the Ottoman Empire. After that, the town became known affectionately as 'Little Vienna of the East'. Four hundred years of Turkish rule had left a few traces on the city: the Turkish baths, the Turkish well and bridge, a tradition of delicious strudels (thought to have derived from filo pastry) and coffee. A legacy of this is my grandmother's Turkish-style coffee pot which now belongs to me. The strength of Austrian national feeling amongst the German-speaking inhabitants of Czernowitz cannot be underestimated. My family, like most people from Czernowitz, continued to regard themselves as Austrian citizens even after the collapse of the Austro-Hungarian Empire in 1918.

Martha and Theodor's son, my Uncle Reinhold, was born in 1908, by which time Emperor Franz Joseph had been ruling for sixty years. In his autobiography *Mes quatre vies*, Uncle Reinhold remembers cheering the old Kaiser sometime during the First World War when he appeared on the balcony of the Schönbrunn Palace. Soon after, in 1916, Reinhold attended his funeral. During the Kaiser's reign, the people of Czernowitz enjoyed a sense of apparently unshakeable security. Loyalty towards the monarch was summed up in the well-worn phrase '*Kaiserlich und Königlich*' – 'Imperial and Royal' – used to describe the values of upstanding citizens.

In the latter part of the nineteenth century and the first two decades of the twentieth, Czernowitz, under Habsburg rule, was an extraordinarily multicultural and multi-ethnic place with populations of Poles, Germans, Ukrainians (referred to at that time as Ruthenians), Armenians, Romanians, Hungarians, Gypsies, Slovaks and Jews. After the revolution of 1917, fleeing Russians also came to the city. Edith's parents employed a Russian princess to teach their daughter French in their home. She never forgot the helplessness of the poor lady when it came to everyday life – she had been so used to being waited on hand and foot, that she either couldn't or wouldn't open a door for herself.

Before the Second World War, according to the census of Romania for the year 1930, the total population of the city of Czernowitz (*Cernăuţi* in Romanian) was around 115,000, of which roughly one third were Jews. There were, broadly speaking, three groups of Jews: the observant Yiddish-speaking people, who lived mainly in the lower town, the completely assimilated non-observant German-speaking bourgeoisie who lived in the centre of town, and the Hassidim in Sadagora just outside the city, the seat of a very orthodox branch of Judaism which had started in the eighteenth century. Theodor and Martha Kern belonged to the second category: they never entered a synagogue, spoke German, not Yiddish, lived completely secular lives and were wholly integrated within Austrian culture. Although people from different cultures did not mix much, they lived in harmony and it was considered normal for most people to speak several languages. Throughout the one hundred and fifty or so years of Habsburg rule, there were no pogroms in Czernowitz, and all religions were tolerated.

Reinhold loved going to the market as a child, to see Ruthenian and Romanian peasants in their exotic costumes, unloading their produce from horse-drawn carts. He could tell which nationality people belonged to from subtle differences in their clothing, such as the style of the embroidery on the women's blouses, the cut of their skirts and the colour of their jackets and whether the men wore their trousers tucked inside their boots. The Czernowitz-born author, Gregor von Rezzori, remembered seeing peasant women coming into the Ring Platz in the centre of town, carrying baskets full of eggs on their heads.

The centre of town, with its great number of municipal buildings, was modelled on the grand Viennese style of the Habsburg era, boasting many façades of decorative stucco and art nouveau (Jugendstil) features. There are several particularly impressive edifices still standing, including the station, the magnificent theatre (a copy of the *Deutsche Volks Theatre* in Vienna) and the art gallery. Each ethnic group had its own national house of culture with its own theatre and likewise each cultural and ethnic group had its own places of worship. There were over seventy synagogues, one of which was the magnificent Moorish-style building in the centre of town known as 'The Great Temple'. The inside of the huge cupola in baroque style (which was added in 1880, about twenty years after the Temple was built) was decorated with a blue background sprinkled with gold stars. The eastern influence was evident in the Greek Orthodox cathedral and the Armenian church.

The Kern family lived in a three-bedroomed flat at Number 47 Herrengasse, the highly prestigious main shopping street. The household consisted of the parents, Theodor and Martha, and the two children, Reinhold and Edith. Reinhold was six years older than Edith. Martha's mother, my great-grandmother, Rosa, stayed with the family for periods of time and they also had a maid, Mizzi, who lived in with the family during my mother's childhood. Life was comfortable and full of pleasures.

Herrengasse, an elegant street with its three- and four-storey houses, was always crowded with people strolling up and down, showing off their best clothes and exchanging gossip. Window shopping was popular at shops like *Zür Französin* at Number 16, which displayed the latest fashions from Vienna and Paris. The *Café de l'Europe*, advertised as the 'Rendezvous place for the best society', was on Herrengasse and the *Café Habsburg* was only a few steps away. Here you could enjoy smoked salmon and caviar, delicious Viennese patisserie piled high with cream and good coffee, whilst reading a newspaper (probably on a stick) or journal from abroad in a sumptuous art nouveau interior, decorated with a large, tiled fountain, chandeliers and wall frescoes.

Living in Central Europe, people were strongly affected by extremes of temperature. Edith recalled that there was a huge thermometer on the tower of the Town Hall which regularly rose to thirty-five degrees centigrade or higher in summer, dropping to minus twenty in winter. The River Prut flowed down from its source high up in the Carpathian Mountains around the town, following a long course to the Black Sea. One of Edith's happiest childhood memories was ice-skating on the river. A favourite occupation in the summer was to take a picnic to the river beach called 'Venezia' and swim and sunbathe all day. My grandparents loved the mountains and often went walking in the Carpathians, which were within easy reach of the city. There are several photographs in our family album of Martha on mountain treks, wearing sturdy walking shoes, holding armfuls of wildflowers. Edith inherited a lifelong love of mountains from her parents; her favourite flowers were the small, fragrant, pink cyclamen which grew in carpets on Alpine mountainsides in autumn.

The family usually spent their holidays in the wooded hills and valleys of southern Bukovina, a landscape dotted with windmills and sawmills to service the timber industry, and where Uncle Reinhold had adventures travelling downstream on log rafts. Every summer and sometimes in winter too, Grandpa Theodor took a cure at a small but chic mountain town called Dorna Vatra, where even the bandstand or *Musikpavillion* in the town was an elaborately decorated construction with crenelated arches. The spa hotel frequented by my grandparents was a smart establishment with its own concert hall and croquet lawn. Theodor was a great believer in carbon dioxide baths, which he found relieved stress and lowered blood pressure.

My grandmother's father, Jakob Beiner, was a lawyer who died young, leaving my great-grandmother, Rosa, with five children to bring up, when the youngest was just a baby. She was, by all accounts, a forceful and very warm-hearted character, commanding respect and love. The Beiner family was close-knit, even though some of them had moved away. Martha's older sister, Otilie (known as 'Lili'), had married and moved to Timişoara in Hungary. Jacobina (known as 'Bina'), her youngest sister, moved to Vienna when she was married, and Robert, a lawyer, had also moved to Vienna. A second brother, Lonio, became a banker. The siblings all returned to Czernowitz to celebrate their mother Rosa's eightieth birthday in 1938, a lavish affair for which they hired an aristocrat's cook to do the catering.

Reading through the correspondence between my great-grandmother, Rosa, her daughter, Martha and my mother, Edith, I can see a pattern of nurturing, tenderness and unconditional love passing through the generations. Rosa's contributions in spiky handwriting in green ink were brief but full of endearments, optimism and good wishes. Rosa and Martha often signed off their letters with the word '*Innigst*' which does not have an exact equivalent in English. It conveys most deeply felt devotion and intimacy. Martha often mentioned how her mother brought her coffee in bed in the mornings, ministered to her whilst she was working and how she was ready with soothing remedies, such as salts for an upset tummy. My cousin, Annie, remembered my great-grandmother presiding over a huge pot in the kitchen and the tempting smells coming from it. Rosa took an interest in current affairs and was an enthusiastic player of bridge and rummy. In extreme old age she spent much of her time enjoying the sunshine on the balcony, wrapped up in a blanket.

Born in 1879, my grandfather, Theodor, probably met my grandmother, Martha, when he was at university in Czernowitz. They married in 1906 after he graduated, and he remained in the town with her for the rest of his life. There was nothing to draw him back to his hometown, Burdujeni, about fifty miles away, where in 1907 there had been an uprising of Ukrainian peasants against the Jews. Theodor's father might have been one of those unfortunate people who fled from the town during the attack, only to find their shops looted and vandalised on their return. Theodor took up a post as Head of Latin and Greek in the Gymnasium in Czernowitz, and later became one of the founders of the first secondary school for girls in the town. Although, by all accounts, he was a gifted teacher and highly respected for his tolerance and fairness, he was somewhat severe and remote – possibly even rather humourless. Nevertheless, he was a kind and devoted father, instilling a strong work ethic in his children through example. An upright public servant, he was typical of the people who formed the mainstay of the town.

Martha was an altogether different personality. According to Reinhold, she was vivacious, gay and brilliant. Nearly ten years younger than Theodor, she was only eighteen when they married, and she gave birth to Reinhold just over a year later. Theodor complained in a letter that whilst she was away, the doorbell hardly ever rang. Described by one of her friends as 'genusssüchtig' (pleasure-seeking), most unconventionally for a woman of that time, she travelled to Italy on her own in 1912 to study art in Rome and Florence, leaving her small son with her husband. The same friend commented that lust for life was a trait of the Beiner family. Uncle Reinhold remembered being proud of having a young and slender mother with long blond hair falling to her waist, who was often mistaken for his older sister.

In 1925, as a change from the mountains, the family went on holiday to Constanţa on the Black Sea, where my mother learned to swim. At seventeen, Reinhold was much more interested in exploring the great docks than in swimming and sunbathing. He struck up a conversation with some sailors on a merchant ship bound for Constantinople, as Istanbul was still called in those days. They invited him to join them the next day when the ship was due to leave. When Reinhold put this proposal to his parents over supper, he received a flat 'no' from his father. His mother remained silent. Afterwards she took Reinhold to one side and asked him to introduce her to the captain of the ship. To his astonishment she asked the captain if he would take her too. He agreed, and so mother and son were able to cross the Black Sea to Istanbul and to enjoy a few unforgettable days there together.

Rosa Roth-Zuckermann, whom I met on a visit to Czernowitz in 2001 when she was over ninety, remembered Martha as one of the 'most highly educated and cultivated women in the city'. The late nineteenth century and early twentieth century saw a flourishing of culture in Czernowitz in all the arts. There was an exceptional blossoming of writers and poets in the German language who were mostly Jewish, and a passion for their works among the citizens. The extent of this can be gauged, for example, from the public reaction to the death of the poet, Elieser Steinbarg, when thousands of tearful people joined hands on the mile-long walk from the funeral to the cemetery. The literary heritage of Czernowitz has been commemorated in today's Ukraine with memorials and information plaques about famous poets such as Paul Celan and Rose Ausländer displayed all over the city. In recent years in the former Herrengasse, a new plaque was put up which reads: 'Czernowitz, halfway between Kiev and Bukarest, Krakau and Odessa, was the secret capital of Europe, where bunches of roses were swept from the pavements and where there were more bookshops than bakeries.'

Martha took an active part in the cultural life of Czernowitz; she was renowned for holding a weekly salon attended by up to twenty poets and writers (probably all women) who gathered to read and discuss their works. Sometimes she also organised concert performances. She had a long friendship with Ninon Hesse, the wife of Herman Hesse, with whom she shared an interest in art and poetry. When she returned from Italy, Martha studied at the university and afterwards taught history of art and literature, writing articles for several newspapers published in Czernowitz, such as the *Morgenblatt* and the *Czernowitzer Allgemeine Zeitung*, edited by the well-known poet Alfred Margul-Sperber.

Martha reviewed the first collection of poems, *Der Regenbogen* (The Rainbow) by the Czernowitz-born poet, Rose Ausländer, who later came to be regarded as one of the foremost lyricists of the twentieth century. In her review, which appeared in the *Czernowitzer Morgenblatt* in April 1940, she recognised Rose Ausländer's great gifts, concluding: "Her song, *The Golden Bird*, brings into our grey existence light and colour, meaning and comfort." The photographs of Martha when she was young show a woman of gentle beauty. As a mature woman, she was statuesque verging on stout, emanating calm, wisdom and kindness. She was probably not very happy in her marriage, describing her husband in one of the letters as '*schwerblutig*' – phlegmatic and conservative.

Edith, my mother, was born in February 1914, a few months before the outbreak of the First World War. Soon the Russians had occupied Czernowitz and the family, like many others, escaped to the capital, Vienna, for the duration, as heavy fighting ensued. Theodor joined the Austrian army. Reinhold recorded some of his memories of Vienna during the First World War in his autobiography. He remembered having to queue up for rations. He also went to school where he was bullied by other boys because he was Jewish. On several occasions, he was beaten up after school, returning home with torn clothes, bruises and black eyes. After a while, he decided to give back as good as he got, which resulted in the bullies leaving him alone and ultimately treating him with respect. Interestingly, he reflected that this was a very formative experience which taught him never to be passive. His innate self-confidence was to prove indispensable in later life. My mother's personality and attitude were quite the opposite.

She did not tell me very much about her childhood in Czernowitz. She was born at home and a photograph of her mother looking adoringly at Edith as a baby swathed in silk and lace confirms that she was much cherished and cossetted. Writing to her daughter to celebrate her thirtieth birthday, Martha says, "I remembered so clearly the moment when they gave you to me to hold for the first time. When I saw your blue eyes – they were deep blue at that time – and I stroked your tiny little hand with the silky skin, my whole heart flowed to you." The earliest photograph shows her as a baby ensconced in a mass of exquisite white swaddling clothes, and as a small child, her hair was decorated with a ribbon tied in a huge bow. In a letter to Ralph, she confesses that she was spoilt for the first seventeen years of her life until she left home.

When she was four years old, she caught diphtheria. A tracheotomy, the only treatment at that time, saved her life but permanently damaged one of her vocal cords, leaving a small scar. Sadly, for such a musical person, Edith was never able to sing. Sometimes when playing the piano, she got carried away and would try, but all that came out was a croak. She started learning the piano when she was five or six, and her parents must soon have become aware of her talent. When they took her to her first concert at the age of eight, she was completely enthralled. In 1931 Edith left Czernowitz to study music in Vienna, and apart from short visits to the family in the early 1930s never returned to live there again.

The final member of the household to be described is Mizzi, the maid. It is not clear for how long she lived in with the Kern family, since at some point she got married to a soldier. For many years, however, the first thing she did every morning was to present herself to Martha when she was still in bed and pose the question: *"Gnädige Frau, was wird heute gekocht?"* – What would you like me to cook today, Madam? (Literally, 'gracious lady'.) Martha must have appreciated Mizzi's cooking, as she attributed several recipes to her in her collection. Whenever Martha went on her travels, she left her in charge of the household. In a letter to his wife, Theodor reported all was running smoothly: "Mizzi is honest and worthy. She does her duty and the table is to my taste." He sent her Mizzi's love: "Mizzi greets you and kisses your hands." Mizzi was always involved in family celebrations and social occasions. Martha referred to the delicious sandwiches she made for the salon ladies on Tuesdays. She also made birthday cakes and on Good Friday, a traditional honey cake. In one of her letters Martha reminisced about Edith's birthday, when they invited a group of her little friends, pulled out the table and Mizzi served nut cake 'as tall as a house' covered in cream. On cold winter days, Martha lent Mizzi her fur coat to go to the market and she was a great support to Martha when she broke her arm, helping her to get dressed and cutting up her food for her. She left the family during the Second World War and worked as an assistant in a grocery shop in Sosnowicz, Silesia. They always kept in touch.

Following the dissolution of the Austro-Hungarian Empire

after the First World War, the regions of Bukovina, Hungarian Transylvania and Bessarabia (previously part of Russia) were all transferred to Romania. This included Czernowitz which was renamed '*Cernăuţi*'. Street names were also changed: Herrengasse was now called 'Iancu Flondor' Street, after a prominent contemporary Romanian nationalist. However, as far as ordinary citizens were concerned, they were still Austrian, and nothing had changed. Even in the early 1930s, Martha still referred to visiting her sister Lili in Timişoara, as going to Hungary. Although people remained oblivious to the ending of the Habsburg era and the Austrian way of life, the inexorable consequences were gathering momentum.

The early years of Romanian rule in the 1920s were peaceful and prosperous, and the insidious corruption within the establishment which favoured Romanians above all other nationalities could be overlooked by most people. In Romania itself, nationalism and anti-Semitism were endemic; Aharon Appelfeld, the well-known Jewish author, born in 1932 in Czernowitz, comments that his father had left Bucharest because of anti-Semitism. When the Romanians took over, one of their first legislative acts was to make people apply for Romanian citizenship.

By 1924, Romanian had been established as the official language. The last performance in German at the State Theatre was in 1922, when Romanian students stormed onto the stage, forcing the actors to stop. Henceforth plays in German could only be performed in the German House, in the former Herrengasse, where my family were living. Bukovinian Jews lost their jobs if it was considered that they did not speak good enough Romanian, and Jews in official posts were replaced by Romanians. Martha started reading the newspaper in Romanian, and the language of all educational institutions, including both schools and the university, switched to

Romanian. Edith deeply resented this, since speaking German was forbidden anywhere on the school premises. After leaving school she forgot the Romanian language completely. Later in the 1930s, schoolchildren could be taken to the police station and fined if caught speaking German. University places were limited by a *numerus clausus* system which favoured Romanians. Edith never spoke of the fact that Theodor, who was always respectfully addressed as 'Herr Professor', suddenly lost his job at the prestigious Gymnasium, after working there for thirty years, and without any warning, was sent to teach in a Romanian school, the Gimnaziul de felo Carazal, in a small town many miles from the city. In a letter to Edith in 1935, he alludes to the 'restriction in his profession imposed on minorities in their country in recent times'. The *numerus clausus* had become *numerus nullus*, he commented bitterly. Segregation of all the minorities became the norm, each having its own school. At home it was no longer possible to socialise with Romanians or with people of other nationalities, as they had been used to doing previously, because anti-Semitism was now poisoning the atmosphere.

During the late 1920s, the Iron Guard, a far-right movement purporting to be Orthodox Christian, was gaining strength. Now there was overt anti-Semitism, with Jews being beaten up on the streets. Synagogues were vandalised, Jewish houses burnt down, and Jews, intellectuals and people on the left were particularly targeted. Ed Wagner, a young left-wing Jewish optician who played in an orchestra, was tortured and thrown out of a window. He died two days later.

Another particularly ugly incident prompted young people to emigrate in large numbers: a Jewish school-leaver by the name of David Fallik was shot and killed by a member of the Iron Guard. The perpetrator was let off scot-free because of corruption. David Fallik had been a classmate of Reinhold. His death and the scandalous injustice of the trial were important factors in Reinhold's decision to emigrate to France to study medicine. As a very politically aware young man, he would have very likely rejected the option of going to Vienna, where the far right was also gaining ground. He was already engaged to Fanny Ungar, the daughter of a businessman who owned a toyshop and a printing shop near to the Kerns' flat in Herrengasse. Fanny was celebrated as one of the loveliest young women in Czernowitz, with such a beautiful body that she was photographed in the nude. She had also chosen to study medicine. Since, in any case, there was no medical faculty in Czernowitz, the couple decided to emigrate. Both Reinhold and Fanny (known as 'Fa') gained places at medical school in Montpellier. They completed their studies, married and became French citizens.

Edith never told me anything much about life in Vienna in the 1930s. Her six years at the university had not been a happy time. She had worked very hard at the piano, gaining the highest diploma in 1935, but the effort of studying had been at the expense of her social life. She did make one lifelong friend, Friedl, a violinist who later conducted the Vienna Boys Choir. On Sundays Edith visited her Aunt Bina, her Uncle Emo and their daughter, Hannah (Annie). Annie remembered that my mother loved her aunt's potato mayonnaise and enjoyed going for an afternoon stroll under the pink-flowering chestnut trees in the Prater, nearby. Perhaps Edith was too immersed in her doctoral thesis entitled *The Use of Ecclesiastical Modes in the Piano Music of the Romantics with particular reference to Brahms*, to take much notice of political events. However, her decision to leave to study the piano at the École Normale de Musique in Paris in 1937 was surely influenced by the popularity of Hitler in Vienna.

In September 1938, two months before Kristallnacht, Martha joined the European Christian Mission. She did not hold any religious beliefs, which she regarded as a 'form of atavism'. However, like many others, some of whom went as far as converting to Christianity, she probably felt this step was justified. The danger to Jews was growing, and she must have thought it would give her some protection. Whilst she admired the sentiments of tolerance and forgiveness in the Christian religion, her views were modern and liberal. She abhorred narrow sectarianism and what she called 'accursed nationalism'. The most important thing was to be educated, speak several languages and accept and rejoice in different peoples and cultures – in short 'to be a good European'. But from now on, there would be no room in Europe for people like her.

3

RALPH

Ralph was born in Hackney and grew up in the East End of London. There could hardly be a greater contrast between his childhood and Edith's: whilst Edith was blessed with security and the devotion of her parents in her early life, Ralph had the most tragic and troubled of beginnings.

Little is known of Ralph's ancestry on his father's side. It is said that his forefathers had been a succession of rabbis from Vilnius in Lithuania or its environs, where they had lived for several generations. A cousin had gained recognition from the Tsar for his marksmanship in the Russian army, for which he was rewarded with a watch. Relatives had started emigrating from Vilnius from the end of the nineteenth century, when it was part of the Russian Empire. They brought very little with them, but one important possession was a samovar. There is one photograph of Ralph's grandfather, taken somewhat mysteriously in Newcastle, not the most usual port of entry to the country. It is possible that he was on his way to the Yeshiva at Gateshead, one of the largest centres for the study of Jewish religious texts in Europe. The photograph is striking, showing a fresh, youngish face beneath a Tolstoyan beard. Whether family members emigrated for economic reasons or because of persecution is not known. Not all of them left Lithuania, but it is highly unlikely that any of those who stayed would have survived the pogroms or the holocaust.

Ralph's father arrived in England in 1908, after an odyssey of indeterminate length. He was fond of telling Ralph throughout his childhood that: "When I was your age, I was walking across Europe to get to here from Lithuania." During that period, there was a massive influx of Jews from all over Russia, Lithuania, Poland and Central Europe to the East End of London. The Aliens Act was passed by Parliament in 1905 to stem the flow, but it was poorly enforced. Ralph's father, Alexander Lubotsky (known as Alec), was born in 1883 and was twenty-five when he arrived in London. He first went to live with other members of the family who had already settled in Bethnal Green. If Alec really had set off from Vilnius as a child, arriving in London at the age of twenty-five, it would be fascinating to know what exactly had happened to him in the intervening years when he was travelling through Europe, mostly on foot. Sadly, this is another thing we will never know.

In 1912 Alec married Jane Learer, Ralph's mother. The wedding photograph shows them standing in front of a house in Well Street in Hackney, long since demolished, near the site of the first Tesco's. The house belonged to Jane's father, and Ralph remembered his fascination with the fig tree in the garden when visiting his grandfather as a child. Somewhat strangely, his parents were sometimes referred to as 'Mr and Mrs Alexander'. On the marriage certificate, Alec is described as a 'Master Tailor', one of the many thousands of Jewish tailors who lived from hand to mouth, many of them working in crowded, insanitary sweated workshops recruiting workers from the 'pig market' (as it was called in Yiddish) in Whitechapel.

Alec and his family moved to 21, East India Dock Road,

E14, where he had his own workshop, several 'helpers' and a shop boy. It is likely that Jane, coming from an established, anglicised Jewish family, brought some money into the business. Like many wives, she probably helped in the workshop. She was an accomplished seamstress, judging from the photograph of her two sons wearing the fine outfits she made for them. However, like nearly all tailors, Alec struggled to make a living. There was so much competition and the cheap tailoring trade suffered from seasonal fluctuations in demand. The makers were just as poverty-stricken as their clientele. According to Bernard, Ralph's brother, when times were hard, and a man's suit had become dilapidated and shiny from wear, Alec would take it apart and remake it inside out. He spoke Yiddish and could not read or write in English. Tailoring was the best option despite the precariousness of the trade.

Jane, or Jennie, as she was called, came from a higher social class than Alec, her family having already been established in England. It seems that she married Alec to escape from an acrimonious home. Unusually for that time, her parents had divorced. Not surprisingly, marriage to Alec was not the solution to her problems and she apparently resented the fact that she had married beneath her. Jane was an astute and meticulous housekeeper, maintaining a firm grip on the family budget, so that the home ran smoothly and efficiently when Ralph was very young. Bernie and Ralph loved to talk about her large jars of home-pickled cucumbers and chicken aspic. They raved about her calves' foot jelly which, of course, was second to none. When I was in my twenties, my Uncle Bernie decided he would like to take me to a Jewish restaurant in Hackney. He persuaded me to order *lockshen* pudding, one of the delights of his childhood, a traditional dessert made from home-made pasta. When it arrived, he was appalled, exclaiming vehemently in an embarrassingly loud voice, "My mother would turn in her grave if she saw this!"

Jane's beautiful dinner service, with its sea-green, floral design was a mark of her relative affluence and refinement. This impression is reinforced by a photograph of her presiding over a tea table, posing with two of her three sisters, wearing a lacy apron and an embroidered blouse, each daintily holding a pretty china cup. Another photograph shows her standing in a garden with a fancy parasol. A tall, black-haired and dark-eyed woman, my father always used the adjective 'handsome' to describe her. She was 'majestically elegant' when she dressed to leave the house, wearing her fox fur, perfume and a flowery and fruity hat.

During Ralph's early childhood, his parents used to enjoy going out from time to time, to one of the many East End music halls. Jane would sing some of the songs at home: he sang this one to me.

"As the years go rolling by and the kiddies multiply
We go higher, higher, high-yer, the kids meself and Mari-ah.
Now we're going to live in an attic near the sky,
It's twenty to one we shall be in the sun 'ere another ten years go by."

Occasionally, as can be seen from a very faded family photograph, there would be an outing in a charabanc, but probably entertainment was rare, and life a hard grind.

One of the most valuable sources of information in my possession is Ralph's unfinished autobiographical novel. He started it in 1937 when he was twenty-two and continued to work on it for a further ten years. He called the protagonist 'John'. This piece of writing complements the memories I have of the account he gave me of his childhood and adolescence. It also sheds much light on his state of mind and is significant both for what he decided to leave out, as well as what he included, especially regarding his mother.

Jane had her first son, Bernard (Bernie), in 1913, about one year after she was married, at the age of twenty-four. She had Ralph two years later. Ralph understood from very early on that his mother had always longed to have a daughter. In his novel he gives free rein to his imagination when describing her reaction to giving birth to a second son:

"The birth had been severe, and they had to call in a specialist and then they took the child away. Soon she was well enough to have the baby. As they passed it over to her it urinated, and she knew from the jet spurting into the air that she had been cheated again. She turned her back on the child and sobbed broken-heartedly into the pillow."

Ralph knew that giving birth to him had left his mother with long-standing 'women's problems' and somehow, he gathered that she had been advised by doctors that on no account should she have any more children because of the risk this would present. He retained early memories of his mother douching herself at night, which must have puzzled him as a child. Later, he realised that this was probably a method of contraception. Whether or not she suffered the bitter disappointment he described in his novel at having a second son, Ralph soon became her favourite. She let his hair grow into long blond curls like a girl's. All his life he treasured the memory of their intimacy when he sat on her lap. He was undoubtedly a mummy's boy.

The opening sentence of Ralph's novel boldly states the theme of the fictionalised autobiography: "The stigma of abnormality was stamped on him at birth". Ralph writes that, from an early age, John liked girls' toys and pursuits and wanted to wear bracelets and necklaces. He wheeled a toy pram in the street until he realised that this was not what was expected from a boy. Ralph describes John as a sickly child. Indeed, the photograph taken of his class at Dingle Lane

Elementary School in Poplar shows Ralph as the puniest little bundle of skin and bone of all. He remembered his mother taking him to The London Hospital to have tar baths and his parents forcing him to have a weekly dose of detestable cod liver oil. To persuade him to take it, his father promised to give him a penny once he had finished the bottle. Once he had earned his penny, they made him spend it on another bottle of the foul stuff. Remarkably, however, Ralph eventually grew to the height of 6ft 3 inches (1 metre 90cm)!

Unlike Ralph, Bernie was a proper street kid who joined a gang and was tough enough to stand up for himself. He defended Ralph – whom he referred to as 'Boobah' (Yiddish for 'little doll') – from the other children who bullied him at every opportunity. They picked on him because of his physical weakness, because he was different and because they did not like the fact that he was good at his lessons. He also always spoke proper English, which he probably learnt from his mother, unlike Bernie, who spoke cockney like the other boys. Ralph did not take to any sports. Perhaps he regretted that he never learnt to swim but he always blamed this on the aversion he had developed to the Poplar Baths after a dead body was discovered in the pool.

Both Ralph and Bernie adored their elementary school teachers who were completely dedicated to their work. Ralph retained a lifelong memory of an idyllically happy school trip to the countryside lasting a few days – perhaps to Kent or Sussex. The children had to get up very early and climb up a grassy hillside, so they could watch the puffballs popping up miraculously and be the first to pick them. The East India Dock Road was noisy and busy in those days, as it still is now, so this first outing to the countryside made a deep impression on him. He was so used to the street noise that he found it difficult to sleep in quiet surroundings. The family did have a small back garden, where they fattened a goose. Ralph recalled seeing it being chased round and round when it was time to catch it and wring its neck. He had very fond memories of the family cat, Mephistopheles.

Ralph's novel sheds light on many aspects of his feelings and relationships but interestingly, there is one important aspect of his life he chose to leave out: the fact of his Jewish background is systematically omitted and disguised. He chose English names for the characters, and John's father goes out to work in an undisclosed walk of life. The Lubotsky family, however, was part of a large Jewish clan which was headed by Alec's sister, Rivka Leah. Bernie recalled that she would cook for the extended family (very likely for the Sabbath) using a communal oven. Ralph would certainly have understood Yiddish and learned to say his prayers in Hebrew. As the youngest boy in the family, he had to learn the four traditional questions of Passover in Hebrew for the traditional meal. He was intrigued by having to ask, "Why do the Jews eat bitter herbs at Passover?"

In the summer of 1924, when Ralph was nine and Bernie eleven, Jane was sent to a convalescent home, 'The Chestnuts', at Lancing-on-Sea, near Worthing, where she stayed for several months. The boys were packed off to Limbury near Luton, to be near Jane's parents and relations, where they stayed with a couple called Warden who, it seems, ran a barber's shop. We will never know what Jane was convalescing from. She may have been getting over a gynaecological operation to repair her 'torn insides' from birth trauma, or perhaps she was recovering from a miscarriage or even an abortion, illegal of course, in those days. Whatever the reason, there is no mention of it in any of the letters to Jane from adult members of her family, which leads one to suspect that the subject was taboo.

Some letters from Ralph and Bernie to their mother have survived, showing how different the two boys were and what interested them at that time. Bernie's letters are lengthy and rambling, written in a story-telling style. He does not reveal his feelings but seems keen to tell his mother he is being a good boy:

"I brushed my boots, cleaned my face and hands, put on my cricket shirt, waistcoat and jacket, tie and cap…"

Ralph's letters are short and emotional and include snippets of everyday life:

"Dear Mum, I am longing to go home… I am knitting a skarf (*sic*) for myself trimmed with a white fringe, it is green in colour… I wonder how you are getting on? I hope for the best of news."

In another letter he writes that he is saving up his money to buy a little girl a tea set to put in her doll's house for her birthday, adding:

"… a pedlar has just called, and he has sharpered (*sic*) my pencil for me… Your loving son, Ralph."

He missed her and was homesick:

"Dear Mum, I am making a map of the district around and it helps me to pass the time away. Today an accident happened to the electric cable and it was rather fun to see the assistants shave and cut men's hair by candles… (at the barbers where he was staying). For how long are you staying at The Chestnuts? I hope they can be backed (*sic*) … I am sure you are glad to be rid of me for a while. From your loving son, Ralph."

He spent most of his time reading indoors. Bernie wrote:

"I am getting more brown than Ralph. No wonder. How can the sun see him if he is in the kitchen with his head buried in his books?"

Aunt Kitty, writing to her sister, Jane, complained that she was finding it difficult to keep Ralph occupied.

"Ralph is beginning to get fed up and wants to get back to school. He reads his comics out in no time and then he gets monotonous and keeps worrying me for something to do. I often have to tell him to scratch his behind and scream 'Hooray!'"

Jane returned home to East India Dock Road sometime before Christmas. On Christmas Eve she committed suicide by drinking a bottle of disinfectant. Ralph never recovered from the devastating trauma of this event. Although he never told me the true story of his mother's death, he frequently repeated that his 'poor Mummy had died of pneumonia when she was only thirty-five'. Her last hours were likely to have been agonising, and the fact that the family had called in the rabbi as she was dying also impressed and horrified him. It was only when I was in my forties that a relative told me exactly how my grandmother had died.

The reason for Jane's despair is unclear: in his novel, Ralph depicts an unhappy marriage between Janet (Jane) and George (Alec). Janet's life becomes empty and devoid of meaning. However, there is no objective evidence of what was going on in Jane's mind and the coroner's report from the inquest has not been preserved. George comes home one day to find his wife lying dead on their bedroom floor with an empty bottle of disinfectant beside her. In his novel, Ralph describes the atmosphere in the house immediately after the suicide: "A lot of strangers invaded the house, slept on couches or on armchairs, ordered you about and told you to keep quiet. 'Mummy was only gone for a few weeks and would be back soon.' You couldn't laugh or speak naturally and if you wanted to do anything it was always 'not now, dear.'" No-one, it seems, looked after him or tried to explain why she had died. He pours out his grief in the novel: 'the horrible feeling that never, never again, no matter *what* he did or how much he cried, or how much he cried (*sic*), he could never see her alive again'.

After Jane's death, family life fell to pieces. Alec could not cope at all and took refuge in the pub. Before long, he had lost control of the household finances and started running up debts. The boys were often unfed, and the house grew filthy. The dirt and bedbugs left Ralph with a phobic horror of squalor, disorder and poverty. Alec spent several spells of around three months each in Brixton prison, presumably for non-payment of fines, during which the boys were farmed out to their Aunt Kitty or Aunt Lilly, who were not always kind. Alec, on the other hand, was a happy-go-lucky character, for whom everyone seemed to have a soft spot. Ralph described him as being like Dickens' Mr Micawber – always hoping that something would turn up. Generous to a fault, whenever he had any money he would give it away, usually by buying drinks for other people. Even the prison warders took a liking to Alec once they got to know him, allowing him to bring in his sewing machine.

Ralph loved his father and always spoke of him with compassion. When Alec died in 1953 at the age of seventy, Ralph said of him in a letter to Edith (translated from French):

"So ends a hard life where his pleasures were rare and too often stifled by worry and grief. He was weak but can be forgiven for his various faults because he was good-hearted. I don't think he made a single enemy in his entire life. How many of us could say the same?"

It had quickly become evident that Ralph was exceptionally bright. He had developed an avid reading habit in early childhood, often continuing late into the night by candlelight. Consequently, he won a scholarship to Christ's Hospital secondary school, astonishing the examiners by knowing that there were two writers by the name of Johnson/Jonson. When questioned on this he asked, "Do you mean Dr Johnson who wrote the famous dictionary, or Ben Jonson the playwright?" Despite being awarded a free place, he did not go to that school in the end. The reason given was that his father could not afford to pay for the uniform (which to this day consists of the original ankle-length belted blue coat, knee breeches, yellow socks and white neck bands, all in the original Tudor style and is now provided free of charge).

Instead, Ralph won a scholarship to the highly regarded Raine's School for Boys in Arbour Square, Stepney, known locally as the school for the 'crème de la crème'. Thereafter he was able to continue his education until matriculation in the sixth form, thanks to further scholarships. Bernie, like nearly all working-class boys, left school at fourteen and went straight out to work for a cousin who was a wholesale bookseller, where he continued to work as an employee for the rest of his life.

School was within walking distance of home. Ralph, at the age of eleven, must have been aware of the political turmoil during the General Strike of 1926. The East End in general, and Poplar particularly, harboured many revolutionaries. Indeed, Lenin himself had visited the East End several times earlier in the century and the barber whom Ralph frequented claimed that he had also cut Lenin's hair (in the days when he still had some). During the General Strike, Ralph might have witnessed activists setting fire to the cars of blacklegs driving to work and the army arriving in armoured vehicles to protect the convoys of lorries transporting food from the docks down East India Dock Road. He mentions the strike in his novel but thinks better of informing the reader that John lives near the docks.

"'Down our way', said John *who lived near the docks*, (crossed out) 'we had shoals of students from Oxford and Cambridge unloading the ships. The dockers' kids turned out to stone them, but in exchange for the stones they threw, the students chucked back handfuls of silver, so that in the end they became quite popular, at least with the children.'"

Ralph's surviving school reports show that he was frequently top of the class. His father, delighted by his academic success, would say to him that his good report had added an extra year onto his life. Ralph's behaviour is described as 'excellent'. One teacher noted that he was particularly helpful in the school library. School was very motivating for Ralph; the standard was high, and he was in constant competition with the other bright boys. He developed a reputation as a young man with a prodigious memory and a lacerating tongue. Those who sought the stimulation of his company did so at their peril.

The sixth form was mixed, uniting with the girls' school. Here he made some lasting friends of both sexes, the most important of whom was Henry Rudolf. Henry's son, Anthony, told me that all the myopes – which included Henry and Ralph – were made to sit in the front of the class while the rest sat behind in alphabetical order. Thrown together like this, they began their lifelong friendship. The Rudolfs were relatively comfortably off and Ralph loved visiting their home. On one occasion, Henry's mother offered him some large, glossy black grapes. He may have seen, but had never tasted them before, and embarrassed himself by being greedy.

Having matriculated with distinction in English, French, German and Latin from Raine's School, Ralph was awarded a county scholarship which enabled him to continue his studies in French with German at Queen Mary College, in Mile End Road, East London. Whilst at university, at the age of nineteen, Ralph changed his name by deed poll. He chose the name 'Leigh' because it sounded particularly English, and the spelling 'Leigh' rather than 'Lee' or 'Lea' on account, perhaps, of its Anglo-Saxon resonance. To preserve the connection with his father, he added his name, Alexander, so that he became 'Ralph Alexander Leigh' and persuaded Bernie to do the same. It is easy to understand why Ralph made this decision, given the context of rising fascism: for him it was a major step towards concealing his Jewishness, motivated most probably by a desire to escape from the tainted environment of his early years, coupled with a wish to avoid the anti-Semitism that could obstruct him in his career.

As a group of young intellectuals, Ralph and his friends were passionately involved in current affairs and politics as well as literature and the arts. They would have been deeply concerned by the rise of Hitler and committed to opposing Oswald Mosley and the British Union of Fascists, who were active in the East End. In his novel, Ralph describes John's shock on seeing mounted police using batons against demonstrators. Ralph and his friends witnessed the retreat of the fascists in the Battle of Cable Street in 1936. By this time, they had joined the Communist party and were very involved in supporting the Republicans in the Spanish Civil War. Ralph even went so far as to attempt to enlist in the Republican Army. Providentially, he was turned down because he was so underweight that the recruiting officer thought he was suffering from tuberculosis.

In Ralph's novel, John joins a communist cell. This is a vehicle for Ralph to express his disillusionment with the Communist Party. It seems he could not decide whether the title of the book should refer to his generation of political intellectuals, whom he called *The Onlookers*, or himself as the outsider: *The Onlooker*. The members of the communist cell, all drawn from life, each have their character defects: Phillip is selfish and Maurice, the leader, is 'an unscrupulous idealist', a representative of what Ralph calls 'the gutless generation'.

Ralph and his group of friends, like many young people of this period, also had happy times going on 'rambles', where they could be silly as well as intellectual. His friend, Johnny, reminded him of such an outing in Hainault Forest, when he quoted Marlowe's *Doctor Faustus* describing hell: "I remember it well because Trevor's loathsome bride-to-be pelted you with toadstools when you were already tormented with summer flies…"

The scholarships and grants awarded to Ralph were barely enough to keep him from starvation. In *The Onlooker(s)*, he describes a painful incident which rings true: he had got into the habit of eating lunch in the college dining room where a cooked meal was provided for one shilling. It was an opportunity to eat his fill once during the day. After a while however, a member of staff who had made it her business to watch him, came up to him as he was about to sit down and rebuked him in front of all the other students for heaping more than his fair share onto his plate. Deeply humiliated, he never returned. Instead he made do with 'buns and milk, obscure sausages or questionable sandwiches wolfed in depressing surroundings', frequently going hungry. He remained grateful all his life to his kind Aunt Sylvia, who often had him round for lunch whilst he was a student. There was the added pleasure of seeing his little cousin Flora, who loved to sit on his lap and undo all the buttons of his waistcoat. In *The Onlooker(s)*, John is so poor that he only has one set of clothing. Whenever he washed his underwear, he had to wait for it to dry before putting it on again. Ralph preferred to spend his money on his musical education by going to the Promenade Concerts every night during the season, sitting in the cheapest seats in the gods.

Ralph sat his finals for his Bachelor of Arts degree in French with German in 1936. On reading through the examination questions, his pen started shaking as he realised that he could excel by answering any of them and could not decide which to tackle first. As a result, he obtained the highest first-class degree in his subject in the whole of the University of London for that year. In a letter heartily congratulating him on his success, the principal of Queen Mary College offered him a prize: he could choose a book up to the value of £1 which would be covered with the College Arms.

The pass list for the University of London was published. There was an error which Ralph pounced on with the full weight of his sarcasm:

"Dear Sir,

I wish to acknowledge the receipt of the pass list for the B. A. Examination. At the same time, I should like to indicate, in this otherwise well-produced document, the presence of a source of error and confusion. In the list of those who obtained First Class Honours in French you print my name under the number 8184 together with the designation 'Bedford College'. May I take this opportunity of pointing out that the nearest I have ever been to Bedford College is the Open-Air Theatre in Regent's Park? The error is aggravated by the fact that the said institution is, I am given to understand, confined solely to women students. Although I am personally acquainted with some of them, I am sure you will realise that this is scarcely sufficient grounds for assimilating me to the general student body thereof.

As, I believe, the error was reproduced in the daily press and has already given rise to a certain amount of confusion and a number of rather scandalous pleasantries, may I be permitted to hope that you will be good enough to note the necessary correction in any further printed lists you may issue?

Yours faithfully,

R. A. Leigh. (male)

One-time student of Queen Mary College."

Ralph and Henry remained close friends from the ages of sixteen to twenty-two. For Ralph, Henry was the most important person in his life. At some time, probably quite early on, Ralph had developed a passionate attraction to Henry and was forced to confront the reality of his homosexuality. This was the cause of great inner torment, for which the writing of his novel was perhaps the only outlet. In *The Onlooker(s)*, John, desperately lonely when befriended by Christopher (his name for Henry), is rapidly overwhelmed by his warmth, generosity and the intimacy of his friendship: "It seemed that their friendship would last forever and to them both, that the other was the perfect companion." In what seems like wishful thinking on Ralph's part, he has John move in with Christopher and his family, even sharing a bed with him. He does not go as far as describing any sexual activity. His feelings for Christopher grow from friendship and attachment to the awakening of sexual attraction. Christopher is impressed by John and makes him aware of his brilliance but 'how could he (John) explain that intuitive feeling of inferiority which overpowered him in the presence of others? Even in the presence of Christopher, who obviously admired him and looked up to him?'

In the novel, John is forced to give Christopher up when Rosalind (Esther) arrives on the scene. Being displaced by Esther in real life was agony for Ralph. It took him many years to recover from what he considered to be the loss of Henry, for he could never reconcile himself to coming second in Henry's life. Henry and Esther were married in June 1938 and Ralph did not attend the wedding.

In a book made for her by her children and grandchildren to celebrate her ninetieth birthday, Esther looked back on how she came to choose Henry for a husband:

"I was friendly with Ralph, Henry and Reg. My mother thought that Henry would make the best husband, that I would get on best with him. Reg was tough, Ralph was difficult. I also knew I would get on best with Henry." In the early stages of their friendship, Esther must have been unaware of the reasons for Ralph being 'difficult' – in this situation a gross understatement! In *The Onlooker(s)* Ralph allows John to give vent to hideous feelings of jealousy towards Rosalind which he was unable to express in real life.

It is likely that Ralph did not tell anyone at all about his homosexuality. It was an immense burden for him to bear, a lonely problem with no solution or solace. Through John, he considers his options. First, he dismisses suicide. Drowning in the Thames would have been the obvious way, since, like Ralph, John could not swim: "Suicide was no good, it put an end to too much. What he wanted was an end to his misery, not his life." He was all too aware of the dangers of practising homosexuality in those days long before it was decriminalised. The thought of exposure was terrifying. In his novel, Ralph created a scenario where a drunken older man climbs into John's bed with sexual intentions, thinking he was someone else. The man tries to bribe John to keep quiet, at the same time threatening to smear his name if John tells anyone about the incident. The inevitable lies and deceit of living the life of a practising homosexual were an unacceptable prospect for John. He cries out at the injustice of his plight: "Ostracism, all society transformed into one huge pointing finger... and even if he had transformed his fault into facts, would it have been a crime? The same God that had made men love women had made him love men..." "It was Society that had invented this crime, Society had decreed love, respect, life, for the lovers of women – misery, shame and death for the lovers of men..." John decides that he must become 'normal' – by which he means he would have to renounce love for men and force himself to try to have a relationship with a woman.

In 1937 Ralph accepted a post teaching French and German at Pitman's College, which he found uninspiring. Luckily it was not long before he was offered a scholarship to study for a Ph.D. on the work of Jean-Jacques Rousseau at the Sorbonne in Paris.

4

PARIS

Both Ralph and Edith arrived in Paris in the autumn of 1937 to further their studies. Their first meeting probably did not take place much before the end of that year. Ralph had been granted a year of absence from his Ph.D. course at Queen Mary College, London, to enable him to work on his thesis on Jean-Jacques Rousseau at the Sorbonne, for which he was awarded a scholarship of £150 per annum for two years from the Cloth Workers Company. His accommodation in the *Cité Universitaire* was at the newly opened *Institut Britannique* (also known as the *Collège Franco-Britannique*) which had been planned after the First World War as a symbol of Franco-British friendship. And so, he embarked on what was to become an entire life's work dedicated to Jean-Jacques Rousseau, which eventually resulted in his magnum opus: the *Correspondance Complète de Jean-Jacques Rousseau.*

What was it about Jean-Jacques Rousseau that gave Ralph such inspiration? In one of his essays, he proclaims that many of Rousseau's works are 'electrifying masterpieces' adding that Rousseau viewed his fellow man as 'wretched, depraved, sick and enslaved, when he was destined by nature to be happy, good, healthy and free.'[1] Later, Ralph gave his own explanation: "I am sometimes asked, rather more frequently of late, what made me devote upwards of thirty years of my life to editing Rousseau's correspondence. By now I have my answer off pat, or rather, both my answers, the long one and the short one. Before the present audience, to whom the name of Rousseau can hardly be unfamiliar, it is the latter which seems more appropriate: so here it is. Rousseau is a colossus of European cultural history for three reasons: he was an outstandingly great writer, a challenging and influential thinker, and a fascinating personality."[2]

Clearly, Ralph found much in Rousseau to identify with – brilliant, controversial, outspoken and oversensitive outsider that he was – and there were other reasons besides for placing himself at the bottom of this Everest, which he may not have understood himself at the time, although he was not without moments of despondency. Writing to his friend, Johnny, in 1937, he said: "My work is going as badly as it can. I believe I shall drop Rousseau shortly. I despise him because his political works had no influence in England during the eighteenth century".

Ralph was a conspicuous personality amongst his fellow students at the *Institut*: he was always quick to speak his mind and soon became known for his passion during political discussions. He was also prone to give offence and equally liable to take it, where none was intended. In a long letter to him in French, covering such diverse topics as idealism, materialism, realism, communism, religion and the Spanish Civil War, one of his women friends confesses how she was missing him, especially the sight of him thumping his fist on the table when infuriated.

Women also enjoyed his humour and wit, sensing that he would go far in life, although his tactlessness could be devastating. When a devoted school friend came to visit in Paris, he ruined her holiday because he told her what he really thought about her frock. She was one of several women who lost their heart to him. It is easy to see how their maternal instinct could be aroused at the sight of his undernourished, gangly figure (which he pathetically tried to disguise by means of careful attention to dress), especially when they found out that he was motherless. He was still going hungry whenever his scholarship money came through late.

Barbara, a fellow student (not her real name), fell obsessively in love with Ralph, confiding her overwhelming feelings to her diary, which she later gave to him in the hope of getting him out of her system. He kept it. The document provides a vivid picture of student life, especially that of her beloved. She tracked his every coming and going, recording each outing she made with him and all his dates with other women. She always referred to him as 'Leigh' because his reserve did not permit first names, except with his closest friends. They frequently went to the cinema, the theatre, and to musical gatherings, or played tennis, strolled by the Seine stopping at cafés, where they drank hot chocolate and discussed literature. They even went to the occasional ball. For such impoverished students – Barbara claimed that she had had to live on black coffee for the best part of a week – they seem to have managed to have a good time. She tormented herself with questions about him. Did he return her feelings? She suspected that 'Leigh' was Jewish but did not dare ask because he was generally so guarded about family and personal matters.

Ralph was probably not unaware of the effect he had on women. Later, when writing about the *Institut* and this period of his life in *The Onlooker(s)*, he says: "The whole place was full of people miserable because of sex. They were dominated by it. Nothing else in their lives at that moment seemed to matter." Perhaps he was rather careless with the feelings of his women friends because he was still so preoccupied with his own love for Henry. In a letter to a cousin around the time of Henry's marriage to Esther he said: "When you have been closely associated with another person's mind and feelings for a period of close on six years, it is folly to imagine that you can forget about them completely and get used to doing without him". He wrote to his friend, Johnny, "I must confess that all this love business is getting rather monotonous. Do you know that Reggie (a mutual friend and Henry's cousin) was married at Christmas and tomorrow, H is following suit: while H is standing under the canopy[3] in the company of his fair captor, I shall be at the Chamber of Deputies listening to the stormy debate (I believe the epithet is the usual one) on Old Age Pensions... All things considered, the debate promises to be at least as interesting as H's wedding... Are you contemplating holy deadlock?"

*

Edith arrived in Paris from Vienna in 1937, equipped with her diploma certificate from that city which she had gained in 1935, stating that she had 'passed the examination with distinction, proving a special artistic ability and expertise'. She also brought her doctorate certificate, an impressively large scroll written in Latin. The purpose of her studies at the *École Normale de Musique de Paris* was to pass the Concert Diploma, the final qualification needed to pursue a career as a concert pianist. She was to study under the famous pianists, Alfred Cortot and Yvonne Lefébure, herself originally a pupil of Cortot. Yvonne had known Debussy, Fauré, Ravel and Dukas, and had also been taught by Maurice Emmanuel. No doubt Edith could have continued to study in Vienna, but it is highly likely that she decided to flee from the growing oppression of the Nazis. Indeed, the Anschluss took place only months after her departure. Moving to France was a natural step for her, since her brother, Reinhold, and his wife, Fa, had become French citizens and had settled in Bussières, a small country town not far from Lyon, where they both practised medicine. Edith's Uncle Robert, a successful Viennese lawyer, had also set a precedent by emigrating to La Paz in Bolivia, where he opened a gentlemen's outfitters, selling socks, braces, ties and belts.

Edith must have felt very excited at the prospect of being taught by Cortot, and her parents were also very proud that she was to study under the Great Man, whose fame had reached Czernowitz. He had been appointed Professor of Music by Gabriel Fauré, who himself was taught by a pupil of Chopin. Cortot was also a colleague of Maurice Ravel. Edith felt very privileged to be taught the interpretation of Ravel's music 'straight from the horse's mouth' as she put it. This led to her passion for Ravel and Debussy which flourished throughout her career.

Whatever she might have felt initially about Cortot, she had no good words to say about him in retrospect, because of his collaboration with the Nazis after the fall of France, when he became an active member of the Vichy regime. The character of the man can be deduced from his dealings with Ravel. In 1930, the pianist, Paul Wittgenstein, had commissioned Ravel to write a piano concerto for his left hand, since he had had his right arm amputated to the elbow after receiving a gunshot wound in the First World War. Riding roughshod over the composer's wishes, Cortot arranged the concerto for *both* hands and orchestra. Ravel forbade the publication and performance of this version. Despite this, following Ravel's death in 1937, Cortot played his version in public and even made a recording of it.[4]

After Edith's six ascetic and solitary years of study in Vienna, Paris offered a wealth of new musical and social opportunities. Several of her fellow students, such as Clara Haskill and Dinu Lipati, were destined to become famous pianists. She was surrounded by great musicians, one of whom was Francis Poulenc. Poulenc was a member of 'Les Six',[5] a group of six composers who departed from Impressionist music to explore various new styles. She met Poulenc at the Conservatoire, and must have been on friendly terms with him, for he later presented her with signed copies of several of his compositions for the piano. Whether she met the other members of Les Six is not clear, but she owned pieces by all of them and seemed to like Honegger especially. With Cortot she concentrated on Chopin and Ravel, using their own editions of their compositions.

Edith had her practice studio in the *Institut Franco-Britannique* where she might have passed Ralph in the foyer, but their first proper meeting occurred after she had performed a solo recital there. Entranced by her playing, particularly of Schumann, he rushed up to congratulate her at breakfast the following morning, and in the heat of the moment boldly asked her if she would teach him to play the piano. She agreed. He had been hesitating about learning the piano for some years, because, as he explained to a school friend in a letter, he thought it 'undoubtedly folly at my age: it is for this reason that I have kept it a dead secret'. Edith started giving Ralph regular lessons. They usually spoke French together, but sometimes they conversed in German. Edith's French was very good, since this had become the family language at her brother's house. Whilst Ralph's French was impeccable by now, his German could be rather quaint.

Later, Ralph fictionalised his first impressions of Edith in *The Onlooker(s)*. He called her 'Annette' and set the scene somewhere in England. John, the protagonist, said: "'I heard you play last night. I should like you to know how much I liked what you played and how you played it.' John felt nervous. She looked so different, he thought, as her printed cotton frock, slight and ordinary, reduced to life size her commanding concert platform presence... She said: 'Thank you, I'm afraid it wasn't very spectacular.' The voice was quiet, along with a faint exotic accent."

Ralph threw himself into learning the piano and Edith brought all her pedagogic zeal to the lessons which both impressed and daunted him. He gave a quizzical account in a letter to his friend, Johnny: "My teacher is no less than a doctor(ess) in music of the University of Vienna... and is extremely learned – too learned sometimes, for she appears to think that a complete knowledge of the history of music is necessary to anyone who learns to play the piano. I don't mind for I find it absorbing. At the moment we are investigating the relation of all the modern minor modes to the old Aeolian scales... The other day I was initiated into the elements of the orchestra. The transposing instruments caused me a considerable amount of bother..."

After a couple of months, he reported to a school friend that he was making strides: "I have had eight lessons so far and at the moment am busily engaged in practising an engaging little piece which consists of a simple melody in the treble clef with the left hand supplying the chords of the dominant and tonic as required." This piece was one of the Beethoven *Bagatelles*. Although Ralph continued to practise it for most of his life, I never heard him master it. The intense tête-à-têtes about music during lessons gradually blossomed into friendship and intimacy, as he and Edith started to enjoy each other's company more and more. He would pop into her studio at odd moments for a chat and often she would play him pieces that she was working on. A favourite of his was the *Barcarolle* by Chopin which she played to him late at night on her birthday. It later became 'his *Barcarolle*'. She introduced him to the great works of Bach, such as the *Italian Concerto* and the *Chromatic Fantasia and Fugue* – a truly spiritual awakening.

During the holidays of 1938 and 1939 they went their separate ways. At Easter he went back to London, and she to Bussières to stay with her brother and sister-in-law. She continued to practise as much as she could despite the terrible state of her brother's piano – neither Reinhold nor Fa was at all musical. She told Ralph that she was having to make the best of it – or as she put it in German: "*In der Not frisst der Teufel Fliegen.*"[6] He had planned to visit Prague in April 1938, but decided to abandon the idea because of the looming Nazi threat.

The first time they went out together was in May of that year, when their friendship gradually began to deepen as they found more and more in common beyond piano lessons. During the summer of 1938, when Ralph went to Touraine to tutor the children of a wealthy family on a lovely old French estate, they corresponded very frequently. He told her that he had written to her more often than to all his friends put together. The main topic of their letters, written in a mixture of French and German, was the harmony exercises Edith had set for him which he tackled conscientiously, one letter of his on this topic running to fifteen pages. The letters are rather formal in style, using *vous* in French. Edith's closed somewhat stiffly with, "*Croyez, mon cher Leigh, à mes meilleurs pensées et à toute mon amitié.*"[7] The *vous* remained, but the German *Sie* soon evolved into *Du*. Ralph teased her affectionately, as when he addressed her in German as: "Dear high-born highly educated, gracious Doctor of Music" and when he signed off, "Goodbye, Dear Goddess of the piano", or "your disciple". Sometimes irony and banter were lost on her, leading to misunderstandings and difficulties which they ironed out at length. He complained about her handwriting, while her meticulous corrections of his German made him feel she was making fun of him. She warmly invited him to come and visit her and the family in Bussières, adding touchingly in English: "I want to see you before the last rose of summer." Her parents had come from Czernowitz to spend the summer vacation with their children and no doubt Edith was eager to introduce them to Ralph. However, he did not visit her and her family during the summer holidays despite the enticements of playing chess with Reinhold and looking at his fine stamp collection. Disappointed, Edith tried to understand the reasons for his avoidance. "I know that you make a lot of fun of family gatherings, but you see when one has lost one's 'home sweet home' as you say in the English song, these occasions are a necessity."

The nature of Ralph's relationship with Edith was unlike any he had with the other women who were interested in him. Internally, Ralph was struggling to create meaning in his life. He always considered himself to be an artist, expressing himself by writing poetry. He had a deep need for transcendence, which he found through music. In *The Onlooker(s)*, he cruelly rejects Miriam, a character who is in love with him, drawn from an amalgamation of women in his life at that time. Comparing her to 'Annette' (the Edith character) he says "Well, Annette is an artist... she has introduced me to vast new continents of beauty... let's be frank, compared to her, what can you give me?"

When they returned to Paris after the summer holidays, they started going out together more and more. Edith invited Ralph to Cortot's inaugural concert for the term, in which he played the Chopin *Ballades*. Barbara noted in her diary that 'Leigh' and 'Mlle Kern' seemed to be seeing each other a lot at the *Institut*: there were frequent comings and goings between rooms 63 and 96, and they also seemed to have a date to go out every Friday. She was sure they must be engaged. Consumed with jealousy, she also observed that Mlle Kern was taking great care of her appearance.

They must have seemed an odd couple: almost the same age (he was twenty-three and she a year older) they were complete opposites in many ways. Edith was just over five feet tall, reaching up to Ralph's shoulder, blonde, very fair-skinned and tending to plumpness. Although generally timid and mild, with an air of trusting innocence, her very short-sighted blue eyes, the colour of cornflowers, could sometimes flash with surprising passion. Her small hands belied a remarkable stretch on the piano. In contrast, Ralph was over one foot taller than Edith, with dark curly hair, fastidious attire and apparent self-possession, with which he tried to disguise his unhappiness.

He took her out to *The Marriage of Figaro* at the Paris opera, and they went to many concerts together, including a performance of Bach's *Goldberg Variations* by Wanda Landowska, the pioneer of the harpsichord revival. They often just went out for a stroll, when Edith would have difficulty keeping up with him, often begging him to slow down. For her, the spring of 1939 was a very happy time. During the difficult years that followed, whenever she thought about her 'beloved Paris', the sweet smell of the pink-flowering chestnuts in full bloom on the Boulevard Arago, one of their favourite walks, came back to her often. Perhaps they also reminded her of the avenue of chestnuts in the *Prater* in Vienna, which she used to visit with her Aunt Bina and her little first cousin, Annie.

In the winter of 1938–1939, Reinhold had rescued the nine-year-old Hannah (known as 'Annie') from Vienna. Edith shared a room with Annie when she stayed at the house in Bussières. The child was adapting well to French life, quickly learning the language and sailing through her exams. Edith helped her by tutoring her in Latin. By the spring of 1939, Edith and her family were listening anxiously to the BBC News on the wireless every evening at 7.30. She made up her mind that if war broke out, she would give up the piano and go to a hospital in nearby Lyon to train as a nurse.

By now, Edith had come to understand what Ralph meant to her. Like other women, she was in awe of his intellect and was in no doubt that he had a glittering academic career ahead of him. She admired his passion for political justice and his acute sensitivity to beauty. Despite his reserve and dislike of personal questions, she sensed that he had had a difficult life, which aroused powerful feelings of motherly compassion in her. She also found him physically attractive: she loved his 'mocking smile' and quickly realised that his abrasiveness and cynicism were merely superficial.

For his part, Ralph realised the strength and depth of feeling Edith was developing for him, which made him very uneasy. He expressed his discomfort to his friend, Johnny, in London: "I now play Bach's *Prelude in C Major* and shall be shortly attempting the more difficult one in D. But my teacher has fallen in love with me and things are awkward just at present." Things came to a head between them when he began to withdraw, and then, noticing that she seemed sad, asked her the reason. She had perceived a change in him towards her, and like Barbara, who had had to interrupt her studies because she became ill for love of him, she too was tormented. She wrote him a letter asking him not to buy opera tickets, explaining that she was so upset that she was not able to concentrate on her piano. If only he would explain himself, she would be able to understand and accept the situation. She proposed that from now on they should limit their relationship strictly to that of teacher and pupil and that they should stop seeing each other outside their lessons. Ralph replied: "I received your letter. I have written a reply which on reflection I will not send you. I prefer not to complicate things. I remind you simply of everything I ever told you about friendship and I beg you to believe that mine for you will always be deep and sincere." He signed the letter 'R.A. Leigh' – as if it were a legal document.

Had he been on the brink of telling her about his homosexuality? It might have been a tremendous relief for him to do so, but the risk was probably too great. It was better, perhaps, to hint that things were complicated for him. In *The Onlooker(s)*, the relationship between John and Annette fizzles out because of his coldness and her unrequited love, leaving John isolated and lonely. In real life, the friendship between Ralph and Edith recovered from this episode, but by now, the end of term was approaching and with it, the growing likelihood of war. Late during her last evening, after she had finished packing, Edith invited Ralph to her studio where they had spent so many happy hours together. The parting was very emotional. Then once more, they went their separate ways, he to London, and she back to Bussières.

By the end of July 1939, when Hitler and Stalin had agreed to divide Poland between their two countries, Ralph realised that he would not be allowed to return to Paris to start the next academic year. Despite their private jokes about Ralph correcting Edith's 'dangerous liaisons' when she spoke in French, nothing had been formalised between them regarding any future for their relationship. After they had both left Paris, Ralph wrote Edith another impenetrable letter where again, he hinted at problems without any elucidation, informing her that he felt incapable of happiness, and that he did not have the ability to love because he was too selfish to devote himself to another person. Her response was that she did not believe him and that she felt that he was afraid of commitment and constriction. She told him that they should always be honest with each other to maintain genuine contact through their letters. A prerequisite for this was sincerity: "*C'est entendu, n'est-ce pas?*"[8] This precept would be put to the test during their many years of correspondence.

Their short and happy period of intimacy whilst in Paris was going to have to sustain them through thick and thin. Around this time Ralph wrote the conclusion to *The Onlooker(s)* (which, however, he never completed): "A gigantic searchlight swept across the sky, wavered and came to rest; the stars caught in its path turned pale and fled. The war was putting an end to eternity."

5

EXPULSION FROM PARADISE

When they said goodbye before the summer holidays of 1939, Ralph and Edith did so with the hope and expectation of meeting again soon in Paris to resume their friendship. However, this was not to be because of the onset of war on September 3rd 1939. Ralph was obliged to stay in London and Edith, with her brother and sister-in-law in Bussières. Neither of them was prepared for the challenges to come during the long years of separation that followed.

*

RALPH

After two years of studying at the Sorbonne, Ralph's return to the mundane world of work in London in the summer of 1939 had brought him down to earth with a jolt. His cousins had found him work in their wholesale bookselling business on his return to the drab rented flat in Hackney where his father and brother were living. His letters to his old friend, Johnny, whom he first met at Communist Party meetings, are flavoured with the flippancy of disillusion. "In case you are interested, I'm carrying on bravely in the Metropolis of Empire. In the morning I dig manfully at my thesis, which can now, it is confidently predicted, be finished at any time after the end of the coming lustrum[9] and will appear in an abridged form as an additional volume to the next edition of the *Encyclopaedia Britannica*. In the afternoon, invoices, delivery notes, orders, complaints and queries receive my serious attention."

The onset of war changed everything. Ralph was prevented from working on his thesis altogether, since the British Museum, where he was doing his research, had closed for the duration. Furthermore, his grant and money from occasional teaching for the University of London both stopped when the university decamped to Cambridge. With money as tight as ever, and the familiar anxiety about making ends meet, Ralph was leading a dull life. He began to despair of ever completing his thesis.

Days after the declaration of war, Ralph wrote to Edith about what it was like in London. "Well, then, what we have been predicting for years has finally come to pass – ladies and gentlemen, here we are at war." London was 'like a morgue' – at night there was total blackout; all the cinemas and theatres were closed and the only sign of life, walking up the Strand, was the raucous laughter of prostitutes. An unexpected compensation was the fabulous star-encrusted sky of the fine, clear nights at the beginning of that September, which for once could be enjoyed in London because of the pitch darkness.

Ralph was expecting to be called up at any moment. In fact, this was not to take place for another two and a half years. It was the period of the 'phoney war' in Great Britain, when everyone was on edge, expecting an attack at any moment – but nothing happened. Meanwhile, his friend, Johnny, was teaching in a school in Weston-Super-Mare (which he called 'Weston Super Nightmare'). He and Ralph exchanged cynical witticisms in their letters, reflecting the general malaise of the time, also sending each other poems they were writing. Johnny realised that a large part of Ralph's problems was due to loneliness. He wrote the following, with teasing affection.

"To Ralph, immersed in his tower of gloom,
Afraid to forget the tutelary womb,
Grant chiefly love,
That he may come of age
Into his heritage."

So many young men of Johnny and Ralph's age at that time were obliged to put their lives on hold whilst waiting to serve their country. Having to face the possibility of sacrificing their life forced them to think about its purpose. It was only in retrospect that Ralph realised how happy he had been in Paris, remarking in a letter to Edith in January 1940 that leaving had been like 'an expulsion from Paradise'.

During the first few months of the war, which he described as 'those dreary nine months/that strange twilight of the Chamberlain era', Ralph, overcome by apathy and a sense of futility, could hardly bring himself to read a book. In his letters he does not conceal from Edith that he missed her, telling her that he was thinking of her every day, and that the thought of not hearing her play the piano again was unbearable for him. He started to collect recordings of all the pieces she had ever played to him. He wrote in German: "I think of you and not without the deepest gratitude; our parting has left a vacuum in my life." He was delighted when he received a photograph from her taken by her cousin, Elfrieda, a professional photographer, and was touched to see she was wearing a dress he particularly liked. He told Edith that he was not afraid of dying, although it would be regrettable since, so far, he had not achieved anything in his life and there were so many things he wanted to do. Filled with a feeling of the pointlessness of his existence, he asked: "Does life have any sense if it is not orientated towards something permanent and beautiful like the stars?" What he valued above everything was artistic creativity, yet, despite feeling that this was his true vocation, he felt thwarted and unable to express it. Edith, on the other hand, had a marvellous talent. He urged her to continue to work at the piano: "After the war, culture will continue, and you will be one of its high priests. If you can do for just one other person what you have done for me, you will have justified your existence." He begged her not to leave him too long without a sign of life and so they corresponded frequently during the first few months of the war.

*

LIFE IN BUSSIÈRES

During the summer of 1939, Edith's parents, Martha and Theodor, had made the long journey to Bussières from Czernowitz to spend several weeks with their children. Reinhold and Fa had trained in Montpellier and qualified as doctors in Paris in 1933, when they adopted French citizenship, dashing any hopes their parents had had of their returning to practise in Romania. The following year they bought the practice in Bussières, a remote village of roughly two thousand inhabitants in the south-east of France, about thirty miles from St Etienne, in the Auvergne-Rhône-Alps region. They also served the population of the surrounding villages scattered in the mountains. Access to patients' homes could be very difficult, especially in the winter; when there was deep snow, Reinhold resorted to visiting his patients on skis, and in summer the roads could be equally treacherous because of their deep ruts.

The two main occupations in Bussières were silk weaving and farming, a traditional way of life, unchanging from generation to generation. People were naturally conservative and suspicious of strangers. Fa was the first female doctor ever to have worked in the region. Nevertheless, the foreign couple was accepted surprisingly quickly. Reinhold put this down to the luck of having saved the life of a four-year-old boy with a high fever in the early days of his career. Word soon got about that he could be trusted as a good doctor. As the only physicians in an isolated area, they were forced to develop many skills. Reinhold became confident in setting fractures, conducting difficult deliveries of babies in the home, and performing minor surgery, as well as gaining competence in managing a whole range of common diseases and disorders. Fa assisted him in surgical procedures, such as the administration of chloroform when anaesthesia was needed, and ran the surgery when he went off on visits. She also was competent in delivering babies at home which meant that only the most complex cases had to be referred to Lyon. They worked tirelessly with characteristic phenomenal energy, thriving on all the challenges.

Annie, Edith and Reinhold's much younger first cousin, whom Reinhold and Fa had adopted informally, later described the Kerns' life in Bussières before the war as 'Chekhovian'. The house, situated in the centre of the village overlooking the market and only a few steps from the church, was frequently full of visitors eating and drinking and spilling out into the colourful garden. Annie played with the pharmacist's son whose garden adjoined theirs. Inside, the decor was cosy, with bright Romanian kilims on the floor, carpets on the walls and squashy, comfortable, armchairs. During the winter, the Kerns took groups of friends and colleagues on adventurous skiing trips and entertained them at weekends all year round with good food, music, dancing and conversation into the small hours. Their friends, all from the Catholic bourgeoisie, appreciated their warmth and hospitality and the couple soon felt integrated into the community. The practice thrived, and Reinhold was able to send money to his parents in Czernowitz and to his Aunt Lili in Timişoara.

Edith, quite unlike her gregarious brother, found Bussières alienating and stifling. She could tolerate staying there for brief periods of relaxation but soon became restless with a longing to return to Paris. She refers to 'interminable stays' in Bussières, where she was thrown into the company of people with whom she had nothing in common. Writing to Ralph, she tells him how disorientated she felt there when the clatter of the weavers' looms woke her up in the mornings.

In her reply to Ralph's letter just after the declaration of war, she asserted that she felt that war was justified. She had only to think about the experiences of her young cousin, Annie, with whom she shared a room, to reach this conclusion. Annie was the long-awaited only child of Bina (Jacobina, Martha's youngest sister) and Emo. Reinhold and Fa had visited them in Vienna in the spring of 1938 when they were in the process of trying to leave the city. However, they had left it too late. Emo had been reluctant to move and kept postponing the decision. Being relatively elderly, he had felt that the upheaval of leaving would have been too great and had completely underestimated the danger of staying. Reinhold came up with a plan to save nine-year-old Annie by smuggling her into France. He and Annie's parents agreed to meet in the Austrian Alps near the Swiss border. Annie's passport had been stamped with the letter 'J' for Jew in red, with permission to leave Vienna for one week's skiing holiday in Switzerland. At the border, the passport control officials proceeded to undress the child in a thorough search for hidden money or jewellery. They found nothing and let her pass. She said goodbye to her parents and got on the train with Reinhold. A friend of Reinhold's picked them up at the French border, hid Annie on the back seat of the car and drove them into France.

Annie had witnessed ugly scenes in Vienna of Jews being manhandled by Nazis and remembered everything that happened on Kristallnacht in the November of 1938. In her memoir she also describes a frightening incident when she was walking in the Prater with her father. Soldiers with swastikas on their uniforms made them join a large crowd of Jews and forced them to process back into the town in a line, with crowds of Viennese screaming 'dirty Jews' and spitting at them as they went past. All this, as well as seeing the humiliation of elderly Jews being made to scrub the streets, Annie related to Edith, who felt that the only way to remove Hitler was by war. Edith herself felt calm and grateful for the richness of the life she had experienced so far, of which the last year in Paris had been the most precious of all.

Soon after the declaration of war, Reinhold was mobilised into the French army. Edith remained in Bussières with Fa, Annie and Fa's cousin and some friends from Paris. There was little privacy, and little opportunity for her to practise the piano, which was still situated in the waiting room. Reading between the lines, Fa, although 'extremely kind', was also very bossy towards her mild, younger sister-in-law. Edith decided to return to Paris to look for work. On her return there, she found the metro service much reduced and the *Institut Franco-Britannique* shut, as it had been requisitioned by the army. Finding work was next to impossible as all doors were closed to foreigners. She returned to Bussières with leaden feet.

Meanwhile, she had also applied to the hospital in Lyon to do a four-month training course as a nurse. Like Ralph, she was impatient to play her part in the war against Hitler even though, as she admitted, working as a nurse would mean abandoning the piano, an idea too painful to contemplate. The news from her parents in eastern Europe was very worrying. Since the Molotov-Ribbentrop pact between the Soviet Union and Germany, Soviet troops had been pressing on the borders of Bukovina, near to her father's school, only a few miles from Czernowitz itself. She feared they would soon invade just as they had entered Finland the previous year. Ralph was totally against Edith training as a nurse, advising her vehemently to forget this 'grotesque' idea, and demanding a promise from her to follow his advice. The thought of her giving up the piano upset him greatly.

In October, Edith's desire to return to Paris was fulfilled. At first her parents were very reluctant for her to return because of possible danger in the capital. They only relented because she had the opportunity to study for her Concert Diploma with Alfred Cortot again, since Yvonne Lefébure, who had taken over as her principal teacher, had left the city at that time. Edith had not sat this exam during the previous year as she had originally planned. She had been too distracted by love to put in the necessary work and concentration. The exam itself was very stiff – only two students from her class had passed that year. However, she had no regrets about this: in Vienna she had done nothing but study, and she felt sure that the profound feelings she was experiencing for Ralph were bound to find expression in her playing one day.

Cortot made her work as she never had before: they agreed on a programme of pieces for the whole year, starting with three challenging works by Honegger to be performed in a public concert in January. She described them as 'interesting but treacherous'. She also chose the last sonata by Beethoven, *Opus 111*. Besides her weekly lesson with Cortot, she had another with one of his assistants and a third with a fellow student specifically to address problems of technique.

Edith moved into a house in the university area of Paris that had been vacated by the family living with Fa in Bussières. For the first time in her life she had to do all the household chores herself, including the shopping, cleaning, cooking and laundry. It was a lonely time and she echoed Ralph's feeling of emptiness. She was missing him and her beloved Yvonne Lefébure badly. Happily, Yvonne returned to Paris in the New Year, and Edith was able to resume lessons with her. Each lesson with Yvonne was full of revelations, whereas she found Cortot's approach passionless and over-academic in comparison.

In every letter she wrote to Ralph, she talked of the expectation of meeting again in the coming few months. Since he was unable to use the British Museum Reading Room to work on his thesis, she told him she would be only too happy to visit the *Bibliotheque Nationale* in Paris on his behalf; and if she could occupy the seat he had used when he was there, it would help them to feel that the distance between them was shorter. She continued to set him harmony exercises of increasing difficulty, addressing him as '*Cher grand-petit elève*' (Dear big little pupil) although she was sometimes embarrassed by his effusiveness about her musical talent. Their letters show a growing acknowledgement of intimacy and their importance to one another. When they exchanged gifts of music, books and confectionery, Ralph declared that everything he received from her was precious. Edith's letters are full of tenderness and expressions of love. She explained to him what love meant to her: loving and being loved is to be 'affirmed and encouraged by the other in our best endeavours. That is the only enduring form of love'. He must have told her about *The Onlooker(s)*, which he was working on, since she asked in a letter in German, "How is 'the Spectator?' Has he seen much since July?" Her New Year wishes for 1940, in which she hoped for a swift meeting between them and an end to Hitler, were written on a postcard showing the famous gargoyle of Notre Dame.

The winter of 1939–40 proved to be bitterly cold all over Europe. In Paris the temperature went down to minus twelve degrees and in Czernowitz to minus twenty degrees centigrade. The letters from Edith's mother during this period are brimming over with worry, mounting to virtual hysteria and full of advice. "You don't have any warm underwear or any warm stockings," she lamented to her daughter. "You can find little woollen underpants everywhere – believe me they aren't expensive." Although snow was still falling heavily in Czernowitz in the month of April, Martha claimed that she herself was not feeling the cold at all thanks to her old fur coat, pure wool stockings and warm pullovers. She asks Edith how she can possibly practise the piano when it is only eight degrees indoors, imagining herself in her daughter's place: "It is inhuman when I think of you coming home to a lonely, cold house where you creep on ice-cold feet into an ice-cold bed. It goes right through me!"

Letters from her parents are full of concern for her physical, emotional and material well-being. There are additions from grandmother, Rosa, in her inimitable spikey handwriting in green ink, addressed to 'My beloved girlie, my rose petal'. If only Martha could come to Paris, she would willingly cook and look after the house for Edith. They all yearned to know more about her life, showering her with questions. Her father begged her not to be so secretive and her mother accused her of being a sphinx. Martha's letter to Edith for her twenty-sixth birthday, in February 1940, closes tenderly, saying that she does not need to formulate elaborate birthday wishes, all she needs to say is 'For ever'.

It was not as if they had nothing to worry about in Czernowitz: Rosa admitted to Edith that they were all living on their nerves in anticipation of being invaded by the Red Army, and that everyone who came to visit them had their own interpretation of the situation. Edith confided to Ralph that she was desperately worried about her parents, and that she feared that once the Soviet Union had invaded Czernowitz, all communications with her family would be cut off. She knew that her parents would prefer it if she returned to live with them, but despite her great love for them, was determined to stay in Paris. If she left France, she knew she would not be allowed to return.

*

MARTHA

In her letters, Martha made light of the impending danger in Czernowitz. They are mostly full of humdrum details of daily life; she talked about enjoying games of bridge (which she knew Edith considered a frivolous pursuit) and gave her blessing to Edith's decision to have a new perm, which in her opinion was high time, since the last one was nine months previously. She continued to host her salon parties on Tuesday evenings, mentioning casually that on one of those occasions, in February of 1940, she almost cancelled the session, as rumour had it that the Soviets could invade at any time. In the end she had decided to go ahead regardless, and fifteen women came that evening. She reasoned, fatalistically, that it was important not to panic and to preserve one's *sang-froid*. The salon itself was an act of subversion, since the Romanian government had prohibited the circulation of publications in German.

As the year 1940 progressed, Ralph and Edith inched towards a tacit agreement regarding a future together. Their loneliness, an acknowledgement of mutual dependence and the gravity of the ongoing war must all have contributed to the evolution of their relationship. Edith stopped addressing him as '*Mon Cher Leigh*', now calling him by his first name. He calls her '*Ma chère Edith*', becoming more effusive with '*Liebste Ederle*' when writing the occasional letter in German. There were no further harmony exercises or discussions about perfect and imperfect cadences.

Like her family, Ralph also expressed frustration at how little Edith revealed about her daily life, presenting her with a whole page of questions. She told him candidly that an important reason for her decision to stay in Paris was her hope of seeing him there. She was also making plans. Once she had left the Music School, if she was going to be able to stay in Paris, she would need to support herself somehow. She decided she should start saving straight away thinking it would be very useful to learn shorthand and typing – anything to avoid going back to Bussières or returning to Romania. Eventually she managed to find work in a factory outside Paris, which involved a total of three hours of daily commuting. On returning to the house, she threw herself into piano practice for the Concert Diploma.

*

In April 1940, Ralph accepted a teaching post in French and German at a minor public school for boys in Maiden Erlegh, near Reading, Berkshire. It took him some time to settle in. Writing to Johnny, he referred to his pupils sarcastically as 'little lambs' complaining that he was living with a 'motley complement of half-wits and spoilt children'. There were several foreign children, including some native German speakers and the son of Calonescu, the President of the Council of Ministers in Romania.

Ralph had brought the photograph of Edith with him to Maiden Erlegh and placed it on his bedside table. He told her that the last thing he saw at night before he closed his eyes was her face with its gentle smile and hint of reproach. All the time he had been living in the flat in Hackney with his father and his brother, Bernie, the photograph had remained in a drawer.

Ralph explained to Edith that he had hidden it away from his father who did not want to face the day when Ralph would cease to be a bachelor, especially if the chosen woman was unknown and unapproved by him. Edith must have told her mother all about Ralph and his peculiarities, as Martha referred to him as the '*meshugganah* Leigh'. On learning that Edith had sent Ralph a photograph of herself, Martha expressed the hope that Edith was 'looking her best with her nice new perm'. She must have set her heart on the relationship working.

Gradually, Ralph came to enjoy his time at Maiden Erlegh, despite the snobbishness and mediocrity. For the first time since leaving university, he rediscovered the stimulation of reading. Under pressure to keep one step ahead of the German-speaking boys, he read and enjoyed many of the classic works of German literature. He also found delight in the countryside, which in the spring of 1940 must have been ravishingly beautiful, and he even had enough leisure time to take up the piano again. Slowly he began to recover from his malaise. Away from the pressures of London, with this breathing space, he must have made some important decisions about his future. He could not help but respond to the tenderness and frankness expressed so touchingly in all Edith's letters. As he put it, in a flight of idealistic lyricism, he 'missed that tender and indulgent friendship which he got used to, quite wrongly, as if it were normal life and not a new revelation of beauty, an inexhaustible pure spring which is a baptism of the spirit'. Little by little he tried to explain to her that he had a problem, which he described vaguely. When he wrote to her about his 'corrupt soul', she replied saying that when she read that, she had to laugh. However, when he started to refer to illness, naturally enough, she became more concerned, including solicitous enquiries after his health in each letter. She worried because he was all alone and there was no-one to collect prescriptions or to prepare medications for him. And the food was inadequate too! "Oh, how she would love to look after him, her Ralph..." – how like her mother!

He had all but decided that he wished to marry Edith and that to do so, he must overcome his homosexual nature. Something at this time must have given Ralph hope of a 'cure'. And what better opportunity would he have to try this out? Feeling obliged to reassure Edith, he informed her that he was physically very well indeed, but that his complaint was due to a '*maladie nerveuse*'. He explained that he had started treatment, which was to continue for several months, and that his doctor had told him that he should be able to see some changes after a month. He did not go into the nature of the treatment which was to achieve such a miraculous result in so short a time. What Edith inferred from all of this is not clear, but what *is* certain is that nothing could deflect her love for him.

The prospect of liberation from his homosexual feelings must have given Ralph unimaginable relief. It is likely that he found a sympathetic psychotherapist or psychiatrist. Not all such professionals at that period viewed homosexuals as morally and mentally disordered. Freud's view was that it was a state of mind that stemmed from arrested development in childhood which, at that time, he thought was correctable through psychoanalysis, although later he was more sceptical about the individual's ability to change.

Ralph was writing to Edith from Maiden Erlegh every two weeks, regardless of whether he had received a reply. Censorship of letters had started soon after the beginning of the war and postal services were becoming unreliable. There were often long delays and letters did not always reach their destination. Sometimes this would lead to accusations that the other was not replying to letters. At first, Ralph made light of this, complaining that unless Edith wrote more frequently, he would completely lose the skill of deciphering her dear, illegible handwriting. As the arena of war grew closer to them, the delays in the post caused them to worry more about each other's safety. Meticulous archivist that he was, Ralph started to note down the date he replied to each letter from Edith and the date he received any letter from her. He also wrote on the envelope, for the benefit of the censor 'in French/*en français*'. The feeling of a censor looking over their shoulder and the long wait for the answers to their questions must have inhibited the flow of the dialogue in their correspondence, making it more and more difficult to exchange ideas. Still, the censors would have had their work cut out trying to read Edith's handwriting.

Edith had moved to a hotel in Paris where she arranged to have a piano installed. It was far more comfortable and convenient than the house she had been living in and had the added advantage of greatly reducing the commuting time to work. Ralph had decided that he would visit Edith in Paris as soon as possible. She worked by day and practised the piano in the evenings, waiting for him to come. At first, they talked about Easter, then Whitsun and finally settled on the summer holidays when he knew he would be able to get away from school and make the arrangements in time. She was glad that he had not managed to visit at Whitsun as there had been several alerts in Paris at that time and everyone was getting nervous.

By May 1940, the Germans had advanced through Belgium to northern France. This resulted in a huge influx of refugees arriving in Paris, where buses were requisitioned to transport them. Ralph realised that it was inevitable that the Germans would enter Paris and that he would not be given permission to go there after all. By early June, Ralph had become seriously worried about Edith: there had been air raids on the city, killing and injuring hundreds of people. Apparently, the bombing had taken most Parisians by surprise. On June 6th 1940, when Edith was at work in the office of her factory, five bombs fell onto a field about twenty metres outside the building. There was no time to go down to the air-raid shelter, so Edith had to stay in the office. As she heard the window glass shattering, she thought her last moments had come. She does not say whether she ducked under a piece of furniture or whether she was rooted to the spot with fear. For about fifteen minutes, she remained there thinking she was about to be killed. She ends her account of this to Ralph with the comment, "What a pity it would be to die then, only weeks before we had planned to meet again!"

Edith also had some good news to share with Ralph in this letter. Quite remarkably, despite the exhaustion of commuting to work at the factory, and despite the strain of the impending German invasion, she had managed to pass the first part of the Concert Diploma. This meant that she could now leave Paris as she would be free to study for the second part wherever she wished. She had three choices. To leave Paris and go to Bordeaux, where her factory was relocating after the bombardment, to return to Bussières, where her relations had found her a job, or to stay in Paris. With complete disregard for her own safety, she told Ralph that if she knew that she would see him again she would gladly suffer another bombardment. Her brush with death emboldened her to exclaim, "I *must* see you. More than ever I have been feeling this during the last few days, so full of emotion!"

As soon as Ralph received Edith's letter about the bombardment, he wrote back exhorting her to leave Paris immediately, promising to follow her wherever she went. Then, on hearing about the fall of Paris, Ralph sent a telegram to Bussières asking Edith to marry him. It took a whole month to arrive. Although her eventual reply overflowed with joy, she still addressed him as '*vous*'! "I have never felt such profound happiness, and this happiness persists and completely overwhelms me." She immediately set about improving her English, telling him that she was looking forward to becoming *his* pupil from now on. The letter ends "I am confident and happy."

6

UNCERTAINTY

That Edith succeeded in leaving Paris on June 12th 1940, just two days before the Germans entered the city, must have been a matter of sheer luck. Later, she wrote to Ralph telling him a little of the panic of that day; when she left her lodgings, there were no taxis to be found. The few that had been running were charging a fortune, and soon disappeared because the petrol had run out. Edith was obliged to drag her heavy luggage along by herself as fast as she could. When, after a short time, this became too much for her, she opened it in a frenzy, allowing the contents to tumble out pell-mell onto the pavement. Leaving piles of possessions behind, she took the trouble to salvage the photograph of Reims Cathedral, a gift from Ralph, all the letters he had sent and all the notes he had put into her pigeon-hole, realising later that she had clean forgotten to pack her diploma certificate.

Edith must have been caught up in the crowds of Parisians and refugees in their millions fleeing from German-occupied northern France, all trying to leave Paris at the same time, using any means they could to form 'a river of cars, hearses, horse-drawn drays, prams, wheelbarrows, herds of animals'[10] all heading south. All this took place in a terrific heatwave too. The inhabitants of Paris were surprisingly unprepared for the German invasion, despite the steady advance of German forces through the Low Countries and the north-east of France. We will never know how Edith managed to scramble onto one of the trains, already full to bursting point. Once on board, the terror continued, as trains leaving for the south and west were easy targets for German and Italian aerial bombardment. A bicycle would have been much safer on that day.

Thankfully, Edith was spared the sight of German tanks rolling into Paris and German soldiers marching towards the Arc de Triomphe, the ubiquitous swastikas flying over public buildings and the German military bands playing Beethoven under the chestnut trees in the Tuileries Gardens. She did well to leave before the occupation, for people caught trying to escape from Paris afterwards were imprisoned and there were notices everywhere depicting threatening skulls and crossbones to warn people against this.

On hearing the news of the occupation of Paris, Ralph was naturally highly alarmed. Not knowing what had happened to Edith, he wrote to the manager of the factory where she had worked, to see if she had transferred with the staff to Bordeaux. However, he guessed correctly that she had most likely made her way back to Bussières. Edith must have arrived to find an empty house, since Fa had taken Annie to safety in the Dordogne, where they spent the summer with friends. Reinhold was still serving as a doctor in the French army and at that time was collecting a dying friend who needed treatment from a place near the Swiss border. He remembered that the roads were blocked with the flood of refugees and troops heading towards the south and west of France.

On June 22nd 1940, the eighty-four-year-old Field Marshal Pétain, still popular because of his successful command of French forces against the Germans at the Battle of Verdun in 1916, signed the armistice with the Germans. He was put in charge of the 'free zone' and installed in the government headquarters at Vichy, some one hundred and fifty kilometres north-west of Bussières. Reinhold returned to Bussières in August 1940, having been discharged from the army with a glowing report. People took little notice of the rise of Hitler in this remote little town of silk weavers and farmers, who remained appreciative of the Kerns as their family doctors. Their reputation had soared after Fa, who had completed a Diploma of Child Health at Lyon, had persuaded families to immunise their children against diphtheria. Two years later there had been an epidemic of the disease in the area, killing several babies from neighbouring villages, whilst in Bussières there was not a single fatality. The Kerns were then given the task of organising immunisation against diphtheria for all the children in the region.

With the introduction of rationing in September 1940, much of the population had to make do with a diet dominated by Jerusalem artichokes and boiled swedes – not so the Kerns, who received precious gifts from grateful farmers of butter, eggs, cheese and poultry. Having been French citizens since 1933, and feeling so valued in their community, Fa and Reinhold thought they had their own immunity – the immunity from anti-Semitism, but of course, no Jew was safe in Europe now.

The stock market crash of 1929 and the ensuing years of economic depression which had strengthened fascism in their native Romania, had also catalysed right-wing feeling in France. The Depression had increased competition amongst doctors for patients who had less money to pay for their services, to the extent that in Paris in 1935, students from all the medical schools went on strike with the slogan, '*La France aux Français*'. Whilst not worrying about their own safety, Reinhold and Fa took the precaution of protecting their future adopted daughter and cousin, Annie, by having her baptised. Annie duly went through the ceremony, during which she was christened 'Elizabeth'. Her memory of the whole occasion is that she felt completely detached and alienated. Her mother, Bina, in Vienna, and her aunt, Edith's mother, Martha, in Czernowitz, discussed the pros and cons of the christening in their letters. Whilst Bina felt unhappy about it, because she thought it would have the effect of making her daughter feel a loss of identity or, as she put it, 'internally homeless', Martha was more pragmatic, having herself already joined the European Christian Mission in September 1938.

Within a few weeks of the German occupation, posters had appeared in Paris, stating 'Our enemy is the Jew'. Jewish shop windows were stoned and smashed, and the contents looted. The Vichy government lost little time before adopting anti-Jewish measures. The reactionary, conservative and traditional Pétain also put in train the repression of other minorities, including foreigners, communists and homosexuals. By the end of August 1940 the Vichy government had passed a law removing penalties for anti-Semitic defamation. October of that year saw the beginning of more severe measures against the Jews, excluding them from some public offices and interning foreign Jews into newly established camps, simply because they were Jewish.

*

During the latter half of 1940, Europe was in such turmoil that postal communication became increasingly difficult and sometimes impossible. There are great gaps and silences in the correspondence between Ralph and Edith, and Edith and her parents. It was certainly a time of intense anguish and worry. News from Vienna about the activities of the Gestapo was a constant source of anxiety in relation to Annie's parents who were still there.

The surviving letters from Martha to Edith are frustratingly uninformative and sometimes superficial and bland. Doubtless this was because she could feel the scrutiny of the censor looking over her shoulder as she wrote and was also always at pains to reassure her daughter that everything was all right. Edith must have sensed the fear and insecurity that lay beneath the platitudes. Sometime before the Soviet invasion of Bukovina, Martha wrote to Edith telling her that they were still living in their flat, implying that this could change at any time. Following the arrival of the Soviets in Czernowitz on June 28th 1940, Edith received no further letters from her parents until the end of 1941.

During the summer of 1940, while the Germans were deliberating about invading Britain, Ralph and Edith wrote to each other frequently. However, communication became increasingly difficult, especially after July, when diplomatic relations between Vichy and Britain were severed, after the British had sunk a large part of the French fleet off the coast of Algeria, killing over one thousand French sailors.[11]

Ralph started to implement a system of tracking letters caught up in what he called 'the postal labyrinth', noting down in table form the date of writing, sending and receiving letters to and from Edith and keeping drafts in indecipherable scribble with many crossings out, as well as fair copies of his own letters. All this is very helpful for understanding his point of view. Sadly, many of Edith's thoughts, feelings and experiences have not survived. Letters often travelled by a tortuous route, sometimes via known intermediaries in Switzerland, Spain, Yugoslavia or Lisbon. One letter from Edith, dated December 1940, arrived six months later. Letters were returned, months after posting, with the censor's signature and a number stamped on the envelope, and sometimes also the words, "Save wastepaper, metal, bones, rag." Such unreliability and delay made any dialogue between Ralph and Edith very difficult, particularly as they always seemed to be one step behind the ever-changing international situation. Any allusion to politics had to be approached obliquely if at all; it was as if Edith and Ralph were trying to attract each other's attention by waving in a blizzard.

During this period, Edith and Ralph were attempting to grapple with important decisions about their future. Initially, after the fall of Paris, it had been assumed between them that she would come to England. Edith described staying in Bussières as like serving a prison sentence without a date for her release. Burning with impatience to be reunited with Ralph in his 'rich and powerful country', she felt that her whole life was in suspension. She threw herself into studying English with great determination and the help of a phonetic dictionary. Having learned Latin, been forced to learn Romanian and already mastered French, she was well used to studying languages and was pleased with her progress. She confessed to Ralph that she was having some difficulty with her accent and pronunciation especially of the letter 'r', and that prepositions were poisonous! In a more sombre tone, Edith reported that Reinhold's situation had 'become uncertain' and that she had not been able to find work. She was alluding to the looming probability of the withdrawal from him and Fa of the right to practise as doctors.

*

Ralph was still teaching, holed up in the sheltered environment of the minor public school at Maiden Erlegh in Berkshire, except in the school holidays when he returned to London. His friend, Johnny, had joined the R.A.F. in October while Ralph was still waiting to be called up. He informed Johnny that he was writing stories for comics such as *The Dandy*. During the summer holidays he continued with *The Onlooker(s)*. The tranquillity of his uneventful life must have seemed somewhat surreal when the people he cared about were facing such danger. The correspondence between Ralph and Johnny became less flippant as the Blitz raged. Ralph must have expressed his concern for Johnny, to which he replied, "Again, about my wings. Why must you force me to this Rupert Brookish declaration? You can't win wars without loss of life and for myself, I don't mind now that the cause is reasonably justified."

With the increase of anti-Jewish measures by the Vichy government, Edith realised that she must leave France as soon as possible. Her greatest hope, of course, was still to go to London, but she was now considering all her options. It was in November 1940, in a letter in which she addressed Ralph as '*tu*' for the first time, that she put all her cards on the table. She asked him to provide an official reason to the authorities for her going to England, so that she could be granted a visa. She would also need to obtain Spanish and Portuguese visas to be able to travel to Lisbon. The most problematic part of the journey to England would be paying for a flight from Lisbon, as it was not permitted to take more than small sums of money out of France. Ralph would have to arrange for her to collect the money in Lisbon. She was careful not to make demands on Ralph, telling him that 'whatever you decide you can count on my understanding'.

She had also considered returning to Czernowitz, as she still possessed a Romanian passport. Prior to the Soviet invasion, her mother had encouraged this. Martha herself was working in the City Art Gallery and thought there would be many opportunities for Edith to further her musical career in the city. Once it became clear that the Soviet occupation was inevitable, Martha changed her mind. As much as she would have loved to have been reunited with her daughter, she was able to put Edith's happiness first. She realised that once Edith stepped inside the Soviet Union, it would be difficult to get out, and this would be the end of her relationship with 'her Ralph'.

When Edith finally received Ralph's response to her proposal, it was not what she had been hoping for. Things had changed since the fall of Paris, and now the Blitz was terrorising London. He was not at all sure what the best course of action was for Edith. Coming to London would be far too dangerous. At the time of writing he was interrupted by an air-raid siren and the flat had already suffered from bomb damage. Taking responsibility for her safety would be too much for him – it might even cause him to break down. There was no guarantee that she would be able to find work, and she would have nowhere to live, since he would only be free from school duties at weekends. In any case, he might be called up at any time. She certainly would not want to stay with his father and brother, who he described uncharitably as 'neither pleasant nor cultivated'. She would be isolated and lonely, since they could not speak French or German. Since he had no way of supporting her, she might starve. Edith dismissed all these arguments: she was confident that she would cope. She could always stay with her cousin, Elf, who had successfully emigrated to London from Vienna. To her the choice was simple: she would undergo any risk to be with Ralph.

It is difficult to interpret Ralph's reaction and his advice to Edith to return to her family in Czernowitz where, he explained, he felt she would be safer. He assured her that he would come and collect her after the war, which he estimated would go on for a further three years. He suggested that he could even go and live in Bukovina and marry her there. Surely, she would be happier living with her mother (whom he was beginning to regard as 'their mother') rather than living alone in a strange country? At this point he allowed a moment of doubt to enter his argument asking, "Will we be able to forecast what we might be feeling in three years' time? Do I have the right to your heart, on the basis of a memory without a future?" With the end of 1940 approaching, Edith continued to be tossed about emotionally on a vast sea of statelessness, not knowing where to go or how to plan. During periods when Ralph did not receive any news from her, for all he knew she could have left Bussières and returned to Czernowitz after all.

In each of her letters to Ralph, Edith inquired after his health. His replies became increasingly equivocal. He reported that although his physical health remained excellent, he despaired of a complete cure for his psychological problem, even though his doctor did not wish to confirm this in so many words. The condition had become less intense but was still present. He warned her that it could affect their love life. Somewhat disingenuously he wrote: "Now you know everything, or more or less everything; you can decide (what to do) with full knowledge of the situation."

It is impossible to know what Edith was able to deduce from this enigmatic pronouncement. Did she guess that he was telling her that he was homosexual? Edith was certainly very naïve in sexual matters. Ralph was, and remained, the only man she ever had any romantic feelings for in her entire life. But what Edith lacked in sexual experience, she may not have lacked in imagination. It is also quite possible that she discussed the situation with her brother or, possibly, woman to woman with her sister-in-law – after all, both Reinhold and Fa were doctors. She did not care what his problem was. Fervently, she declared her unconditional and everlasting devotion. "For me, *there is nothing* that could possibly affect my feelings for you. I will wait for you until the end of my days. Do not be afraid of telling me completely frankly what you think is the best solution for us."

Ralph's assurances of his feelings for her, although sincere, were not what they seemed. He told her she should never be in any doubt that she was the only woman he had ever thought of marrying. The qualities of her mind and heart that attracted him to her were strong enough to withstand the test of time. One cannot help feeling that the unresolvable issue of his sexuality prevented Ralph from finding a way for Edith to join him in London. When he had proposed to her, he had still had hope of a 'cure'. Now he foresaw that this was not going to happen.

*

Towards the end of 1940, during the coldest winter ever recorded in France, made even less bearable by the absence of coal, the worst fears in the Kern household began to be realised. It had become inevitable that Reinhold and Fa were going to be banned from practising medicine. Sure enough, in March 1941, a letter signed by Field Marshal Pétain arrived confirming this. Shortly before this, the Kerns had received a letter revoking their French citizenship. The reason stated in the second letter was that it was necessary to protect jobs for the many unemployed doctors who were French nationals. However, Reinhold and Fa were loved and respected by their colleagues, who mounted an appeal against the ruling. Four of them tried to petition Pétain in Vichy, only to be refused a hearing. One of these colleagues, a Doctor Eraud, tried to win over the chief surgeon in Lyon hospital, with whom, it transpired, he had absolutely no chance of success because the surgeon himself had just stepped into the shoes of a banned Jewish doctor.

A tragedy occurred on Reinhold's last day at work. A young woman called him because she was bleeding in early pregnancy. Reinhold diagnosed an ectopic pregnancy, a life-threatening condition caused by an embryo growing in one of the patient's fallopian tubes until it burst, instead of implanting in the womb. The terrible thing was that there were no ambulances and no petrol to take the young woman to the emergency department at Lyon hospital where she could have had surgery. As a desperate measure, Reinhold transfused his own blood into the patient. He knew this was worth a try, since, as a universal donor, with a blood group of O negative, he could donate to a person with any other blood group. Despite this heroic attempt to save her, his patient died. So ended Reinhold's career as a country doctor.

The plight of her brother and sister-in-law was an important factor in Edith's decision-making. Having no income of her own, she felt that she could not continue to depend on the generosity of Reinhold and Fa after they had lost their jobs. Reluctantly, she decided to apply for Soviet nationality, presenting herself to the Soviet Consulate in Vichy to start the process of repatriation. On December 23rd she sent a telegram to Ralph informing him that she was returning to Czernowitz. Indicating that she was not angry with him, she wished him a Happy Christmas and a Happy Birthday for the sixth of January. Ralph replied expressing relief. He was sure that she would be safer there and well fed, with a good chance of developing her pianistic career. He advised her to approach the future with confidence, vowing that he would not allow her to 'rot' in the Soviet Union. In preparation for leaving France, Edith obtained a testimonial from her teacher, Alfred Cortot. In this he stated that "Mademoiselle Kern was prevented from continuing her studies because of events", adding that during her stay at the *École Normale de Musique de Paris* "she had demonstrated the greatest zeal and the most commendable industriousness". He signed the document, "*Alfred Cortot, le Président Directeur de l'École Normale de Musique de Paris.*" Of note here is Cortot's implied acquiescence in the political status quo in his neutral reference to 'events'.

7

THE MOUSE TRAP

Since the Russian occupation of Czernowitz, Edith had received very little communication from her parents apart from the occasional 'laconic post card' and one or two letters. One could only guess at what life was really like under the Soviets, during their short stay between June 1940 and June 1941, when the Nazi invasion brought it to a sudden end.

In fact, the Soviets had instigated draconian measures which rapidly transformed society. Before the Soviet occupation, despite the tyrannical reign of the governing Romanians, Czernowitz had retained its Austrian character. Now, Soviet citizenship was automatically conferred on the whole population.

The Soviets struck fear into the hearts of many people. At the sight of Russian soldiers arriving in their white uniforms and white gym shoes, large numbers of Germans and Romanians fled in terror, leaving numerous properties empty. Officials in the Romanian government and police service were arrested, as were owners of big companies, banks and pharmacies, which were then nationalised. People lost their savings overnight, as the rouble replaced the Romanian leu, making it suddenly worthless. With rationing starting immediately, farmers were arrested if they refused to sell their products at fixed prices. People started to go hungry, sometimes queuing for half a day for a piece of bread. Life was not going to be easy in Czernowitz, now renamed 'Chernovtsy'.

The inhabitants were expected to start learning Russian and Ukrainian in the Cyrillic script. For Martha, learning yet another language was not a great challenge. Like many other inhabitants of the city, she was already fluent in German, French and Romanian and she also had a good grounding in English.

During this period, it was risky writing abroad, as the authorities were liable to accuse the sender of espionage, inflicting a penalty of transportation to Siberia. In fact, anyone representing the slightest conceivable threat to the system ran the risk of deportation, which created an atmosphere of dread. This included Zionists, wealthy businessmen, most of whom were Jewish, and political dissidents. Altogether three and a half thousand Jewish people were sent to Siberia. Informers were all around, and people metaphorically 'sat on their packed suitcases' in the Russian tradition of preparing for a journey. In the words of a resident 'everything was kaput after the Russians arrived'.

In the one surviving letter she received from her parents during the Soviet occupation, Edith learned that her father had lost his job as a teacher. The family was forced to move into one room of their three-roomed flat, which they found themselves sharing with a Russian teacher, and Edith's piano was requisitioned.

Nevertheless, despite this dreadful news, Edith was now determined to pursue the application for repatriation to Bukovina. The feeling that she was a burden to Reinhold weighed so heavily on her that she felt compelled to leave whatever the personal cost. Visas, which were necessary both to leave France and to enter another country, were expensive, as well as difficult to obtain, on account of the bureaucratic complexities of the application process.

When she visited the Soviet Consulate in Vichy, Edith discovered that there were delays in the collective repatriations to the East. Applicants from the Baltic area would have to be dealt with first, and her turn would not come for several months because of the difficulties of crossing Central Europe. Writing to Ralph, Edith expressed her frustration whilst waiting for repatriation. It was 'as if she were in a mouse trap'. With no work (apart from housework under the instruction of her sister-in-law) the monotonous days passed slowly. She could never agree to Ralph's proposal of his coming to live in Bukovina, because she could not expect him to make the sacrifice of living so far away from his own country for her sake; their reunion would have to wait until the end of the war, but nothing could make her forget him even if the war continued until 1950! She volunteered that she could not imagine what the problem was that was making him suffer. Despondent and fearful, she comforted herself by playing works by Schumann and Ravel, and most of all by clinging to her memory of him which gave her 'that strange and unique feeling that she had always known him'. She just had to mentally 'put her head against his shoulder' to be 'free of all torment'.

Daily life in Bussières was becoming increasingly difficult. Although Edith did not mention going hungry in her letters, food shortages were widespread by this time and even farmers, who sold their produce on the black market, were bartering food for items in kind. One man living in a neighbouring village claimed that people were so hungry that they sucked their leather belts. The shortage of fuel added to the misery during the exceptionally harsh winters of 1940, 1941 and 1942.

The Kern household listened avidly to the daily 9pm broadcasts from the BBC in London by General de Gaulle, which the Germans had declared illegal. On New Year's Eve of 1940, de Gaulle had encouraged the French people to resist passively, by staying indoors during the New Year's Day celebrations. This proved to be successful, despite attempts by the Germans to lure the people out by distributing free potatoes.

The Vichy government complied with the German policy of persecuting the Jews in its own way. Although Jews were never forced to wear the yellow star on their clothing as they were in the occupied part of France, they were progressively deprived of their rights. On the 31st July 1941, the Kerns received a summons from the Vichy government demanding that they present themselves to the Town Hall to be counted in a census, on pain of imprisonment for one month and a fine of one hundred to one thousand francs. This went hand in hand with the policy of 'aryanising' the professions and the future rounding up of Jews for extermination, which had already begun in the Occupied Zone. By June, having lost their right to practise as doctors, Reinhold and Fa had found work in a small weaving factory owned by a friend by the name of Monsieur Mollon, where Reinhold did the book-keeping. Fa was employed on the shop floor as a warp worker, acquiring the skill of setting up a loom, a painstaking and complex process. Their medical practice was given away to a colleague, also a friend, who allowed Reinhold, Fa, Edith and Annie to continue living in the house.

Towards the end of 1941, Reinhold joined the French Resistance, known in rural areas as 'The Maquis' (which translated literally means 'scrublands'). His plan, eventually, was to join de Gaulle's Free French forces based in London. An official at the Town Hall risked his neck by giving Reinhold false papers: he now went under the name of 'Georges Leblond' appropriately enough, since his hair was so blonde it was almost white. The only person outside the immediate family who knew about his clandestine activities was a teacher whom he and Fa trusted completely.

*

The beginning of 1941 found Ralph still teaching at Maiden Erlegh, cocooned from the harsh realities of the war. Teaching had not taken up very much of Ralph's energy, giving him the time to inhabit a world of his own. He played the piano every day and continued to work on his novel. At this point he was preoccupied with the dealings of the protagonist, John, with the opposite sex. John tries to overcome his homosexuality but finds his girlfriend physically repulsive. Indeed, Ralph's cruel depiction of this person, whom he calls Miriam, seems positively vindictive. John is repelled by her 'violently unpleasant complexion studded with firmly ensconced blackheads: this girl can hardly control herself, he thought in despair, and I can feel nothing, *nothing!*' Perhaps he found it a therapeutic release to give vent to negative feelings about sex with women through the character of John. In a diary of that period, he reveals his ambivalence about the novel, feeling stuck and dissatisfied with it, constantly writing bits and then tearing them up. Perhaps, by now, some of the despair had lifted as he felt his attitude changing. Writing to Edith, he seemed to think that his problem could be kept in bounds but that its seriousness should not be underestimated: "You must not think lightly of the condition I am afflicted with. Just because it's not physical does not make it less important. It's there but not there. I don't want to nurture a mystery that a frank discussion face to face between us could not dissipate quickly."

Ralph was also waiting, interminably, or so it seemed to him, to be called up. At last, in April 1941, he was enlisted into the army as a clerk. The height (six feet two and three-quarter inches or one metre eighty-five) and weight (ten stone two pounds or 64.5 kg) of a proverbial beanpole were duly recorded. On leaving Maiden Erlegh, the headmaster gave him a glowing testimonial: "He is the best teacher of both languages (French and German) that I have had in thirty-six years." Not surprisingly, Ralph soon felt alienated by army life. Writing to Edith from Aldershot he told her that 'he needed her more than ever'.

Ralph could not but feel agitated and impotent on reading about the precarious situation of the Kern household in Bussières. He was still convinced that it was in Edith's best interests to return to Bukovina. However, in September 1941, he received a letter from Edith that changed everything. She told him that life now was at rock-bottom at Bussières. Worst of all, they were all worried sick about the parents in Czernowitz, as reports had reached them that there had been fighting and half the city was in flames. There was no longer any question of Edith returning there. Touchingly, she asked Ralph not to worry about her, expressing her confidence that they would be reunited one day. It was now over two years since they had last met.

On receipt of this news, Ralph applied to the Foreign Office in London for a visa for Edith, only for it to be turned down. He professed himself 'enraged and deeply pained by being a helpless spectator' of the terrible things happening to her and her family, suspecting that she was hiding the worst from him and that she might be starving. He deeply resented the wasted years of their precious youth. Wanting to reassure her about his safety, he told her that, "My country takes good care of its soldiers".

*

CZERNOWITZ 1941-1942

In the family archives, there is very little information about what Edith's parents and grandmother endured during the German invasion of Czernowitz. The period between June and December 1941 is marked with a chilling silence from Martha and Theodor. That they survived was a miracle, but the price they paid can be seen in the photographs of Martha before and after the war. Martha had been an attractive woman, glowing with life and health. At the end of the war, at the age of fifty-seven she looked like a woman of eighty.

According to historical sources and eye-witness testimonials, what happened was as follows: by June 30th when it was inevitable that the German and Romanian armies were about to enter the city, the Soviet army withdrew, leaving via the bridge over the River Prut. The German and Romanian armies did not arrive until July 5th. During these few days of limbo, there was anarchy in the city. Gangs set about looting, plundering and setting fire to the homes of Jews. What was to come was even worse. When the Germans and Romanians arrived, the latter marching six abreast, the first thing they did was to shoot four hundred Jews and throw the bodies into the Prut. More people were taken into the huge synagogue, known as 'The Temple', in the centre of the city, which was set on fire with the people inside, along with all the valuable scrolls of the Torah. The Gestapo set up their headquarters in the Jewish Cultural Home in the main square. During the first twenty-four hours between two and three thousand Jews were murdered. This time, it was the soldiers who broke into homes, looting, plundering, raping and murdering. The Prut Bridge was blasted, and the electricity works destroyed. Eyewitnesses recalled that their city had suddenly turned into a ghost town. The usual practice of making Jews wear a yellow star on their clothing was enforced, and Jewish people were only allowed out of their homes for very restricted periods – sometimes as little as three hours in a day – on pain of death.

The atrocities continued daily. Whether my grandparents witnessed any of these events, I do not know. There have been many accounts from survivors testifying to acts of sadism on the part of Germans and Romanians at that time. One woman remembered that people were made to stand in rows so that the Germans could shoot every tenth person. When an elderly mother was selected, her lovely young daughter stepped forward and asked the officer to shoot her instead. He shot both mother and daughter. The Germans soon left the running of the town to the Romanians, who, whilst generally equally fanatical in their hatred of the Jews, were probably not as highly organised.

In October 1941, the President of Romania, Ion Antonescu, ordered the recently appointed mayor of Czernowitz to establish a ghetto in the lower part of the city where most of the poorest Jews lived. The idea was to force all the Jews into one place from where they could be deported to one of the many camps in Transnistria, about two hundred and fifty miles to the southeast. The entire Jewish population, including Edith's parents and grandmother, would have gone to the ghetto. Even patients from the mental hospital, some of whom were a danger to others, were included. A very few people went into hiding in the town in cellars and attics, bribing their neighbours to secrecy where necessary.

It was snowing on the 11th October 1941 in Czernowitz, when crowds of people, including the elderly supported by young children, sick people and nursing mothers with their babies, trundled their possessions in wheelbarrows or little wagons into the city's 'valley of death'. Fifty thousand people thronged into an area that normally accommodated ten thousand. One witness recalled there being up to thirty people living in one room. Conditions were filthy because the water pipes were cut off, so the inmates could not flush the toilets. In the bitter cold, Romanian soldiers robbed people of their fur hats and removed warm clothing and even shoes. There was no escape, since the ghetto was surrounded by a three-metre-high wooden fence and barbed wire.

A thousand Jews were immediately put into cattle trucks bound for Transnistria. They were forced to complete the last part of the journey on foot in freezing conditions. Many died en route of hunger, exposure, exhaustion or disease. Rosa Roth-Zuckermann, who was aged ninety-two when we met her in 2001 on a visit to Czernowitz (Chernivtsi) was a rare survivor of one of the camps. Her husband, brother, parents and son had all died there in quick succession. I was shocked when, on thanking me for the soap I had brought her as a token gift, she commented that it always reminded her of the soap provided in the camp which was made from human fat. Those who remained in the ghetto depended on outsiders for scraps and pieces of bread which they paid for with money, if they still had any, or gave up their valuables. It was not long before there was an outbreak of typhus.

The one redeeming aspect of this terrible period was the heroism of the mayor, a Romanian named Traian Popovici (1892–1946), who came from nearby Suceava. A man of principle, he successfully challenged the regime in Bucharest, thereby managing to save over twenty thousand Jews. My grandmother, grandfather and great-grandmother must have been members of this lucky minority. Popovici himself gave an account of exactly how this came to pass in a document translated from the Romanian as *My declaration*. In it, he explained that he wanted to save those who 'in the lottery of life were guilty of nothing other than to be born Jewish', which had led to a 'continuum of a thousand years of persecution'. When, during a cabinet meeting, he violently disagreed with the idea of establishing a ghetto, he reported that the colonel in charge of the Romanian military had said, "I come to dig the weeds out of the garden, and you want to oppose me?" Popovici made a passionate speech demanding protection for the highly educated Jews – those who practised the arts, public servants, doctors, engineers, architects and lawyers, and it was agreed that he could draw up a list which should come to no more than two hundred such individuals. Unsatisfied with this small number, he then appealed to Antonescu himself, arguing that the city would not be able to continue to function without essential citizens. Surprisingly and probably thanks to force of character, he obtained permission to exempt twenty thousand people from the ghetto and transportation. As the Romanian authorities were in a great hurry to proceed with the deportations, they only gave Popovici forty-eight hours to compile this list. Popovici then called together the leaders of the Jewish communities and presidents of their societies and asked them to draw it up, making sure that many more people were on it than fell into the category of 'indispensable'. There followed a lot of bribery and corruption. Unscrupulous non-Jews saw this as an opportunity to plunder possessions from the desperate people in the ghetto, by making them false promises of influencing their rescue. A brisk trade developed amongst some gentiles in jewellery and precious items. Some people were able to bribe their way out of the ghetto, by paying the town clerks who were administering the exercise. Equally, the police and the gendarmerie extorted large sums from the desperate, only to force them back into the ghetto to be deported later.

The ghetto only existed for about two months. Already thirty thousand people had been deported, but the deportations had to be suspended in November because heavy snowstorms made transport impossible. Slowly, people were allowed back into the city. Many of them had lost their property and were homeless, and those who did have homes to return to must have felt very guilty knowing so many people who had disappeared. Popovici was removed from office in the spring of 1942 by the Romanian regime, for allegedly giving permits to 'unnecessary Jews'. Later, in June 1942, there were further waves of deportation.

By all accounts, daily life was a bitter struggle during the winter of 1941–1942. People must have lived on their nerves, as properties were still being raided at random. One woman from Czernowitz recalled a terrifying night when soldiers demanded to be let into her flat on the pretext of searching for weapons; they stuck their bayonets into the pillows and duvet with the words 'filthy Jews' and were on the point of killing her and her family, when her mother frightened them by opening the window and screaming for help. It was also dangerous simply to be out and about. The same woman left her house one day to take 'egg coal' (small pieces of coal the size of an egg) to her aunt. A Nazi officer, catching sight of her yellow star, insulted her with the words 'You little Jewish sow' and accused her of carrying grenades. Then he tried to rape her, but she managed to loosen herself from his grasp. It is hardly surprising that, as she told Edith in a later letter, Martha and her mother went out very little that year. The Kerns were lucky that their flat had not been plundered or marked by city officials with a notice in Romanian saying *'Averea Statulul'* – property of the State.

Eventually, Reinhold, Fa and Edith received a long letter from Martha dated 25th December 1941. With the knowledge of what had really happened in Czernowitz, it is interesting to read the account she gave of daily life, in which the hardships are glossed over, without mentioning the dangers. It seems that the family's residential block had stood empty during the previous few months and had fallen into decay. There was no lighting in the upper floors and no running water. Theodor had got up early that day to fetch water from the courtyard. Part of the downstairs had been converted into a cinema and another part a bar. Martha was happy because the previous day she had managed to obtain fuel so that she was able to cook a hot meal. Wood was too expensive, so they used coal. In their one room, Theodor and Martha slept in the bed while Grandmother Rosa slept on the sofa. They had fallen into arrears with the rent, which they owed for the previous six months, and had been forced to borrow money. Both parents were looking for work as private teachers, but nothing had turned up so far.

Although Martha did not allude to the terror and horror of the previous months in this letter, there are some hints as to her emotional state. She told her children that she had been unable to read or to listen to music for the past year. Everything had seemed flat, stale and meaningless. The only reading she had been able to bear was Shakespeare – she was still using the family's complete edition, beautifully illustrated and bound in red, and had just started to read more again – mainly in French – which gave her the feeling of being closer to her children. She worried that their separation might lead to a loss of intimacy between them.

In general, everyone put the most optimistic slant on the grimmest of situations. This was not just, I feel, due to the influence of censorship, but also that each member of the family was trying their best to reassure their relatives. Martha had received several heart-warming letters from 'Edili' (Edith) full of courage and hope. She had also heard from Annie's parents, Emo and Bina. They had moved to a 'private house' in a 'large town' where 'life was cheap and the neighbours friendly'. This was the description that Edith received of the ghetto at Łódź/Litzmannstadt. Of course, inmates of the ghetto were forbidden to mention their living conditions, since had they done so, the letters would have been destroyed by the censor. Łódź ghetto has been described as the most isolated and oppressed of all those in Nazi-occupied Europe, where more than two thousand Jews died of starvation and around one hundred and forty thousand were murdered. In her letter, Martha moved on to lighter matters. There had been a wedding and a new baby. Had the Kerns replaced the dog that died? "Yes," she reflected. "Life goes on in spite of everything!"

8

ESCAPE

It is difficult to establish exactly what was going on with each member of the family during 1942. Communication by letter had become more erratic and of necessity, more guarded than ever. Everyone was aware of strict censorship and the need for circumspection, if not secrecy. Complaining to Edith, Ralph wrote: "how many eyes, I often ask myself, interpose between my pen and your eyes?" For Edith in France and Martha in Czernowitz, the main concern was to reassure their loved ones that they were alive and safe. Edith's parents, now back in their flat in Czernowitz, sent her regular postcards in which they tried to conceal their identity. Her father, Theodor, addresses her as 'My dear friend', while her mother informs her indirectly about her own health telling her that she "saw Martha last week. She has put some weight back on and now weighs over sixty kilos! She is looking very well." For some reason, Martha blows the gaffe and signs off, "I embrace you my little mouse, Martha."

Martha reported to Edith that she had had a letter from Reinhold informing her that he was 'looking after Fa's sister-in-law', who was 'nearer to his heart than ever'. He too was talking in riddles: this was a convoluted way of saying that he was taking care of Edith, his sister, since she was Fa's only sister-in-law. Reinhold, normally so unsentimental, made it clear to his mother that he was protecting Edith from danger: "So much love, so much care is expressed in each word", she commented.

Reinhold was also looking after Annie, who by this time was thirteen years old. The plan was for her go to New York to live with her aunt, her father's sister. At last, after months of waiting, Reinhold had managed to obtain a visa for Annie. This itself was no mean feat; to receive a visa for the United States, the applicant had to give proof of means of support and be able to provide a guarantee from an American resident. At any one time there could be thirty-five thousand applications, very few of which were successful.

He took her down to Marseilles expecting to put her on a ship loaded with children all destined for the United States, only to be told that the departure had been postponed. All the other children were staying in Marseilles for the week, under the wing of the organisation arranging their journey. A strange premonition warned Reinhold not to leave Annie behind. Instead, he took her off to the seaside. On their return, they discovered something terrible had happened: all the children in the hostel who had been waiting to travel to America had been seized and deported by the Germans. That was how Reinhold saved Annie's life for the second time.

*

Writing to Johnny in July 1942, Ralph observed that "the news from Edith is, as usual, desperately vague. I can only guess at her privations, her fatigue, her overwork, her bleak existence among people to whom her presence is a burden. What I do see very definitely, and what I am never allowed to forget, is her great longing and desire for me. I suppose I have become a symbol. It is painful enough for me to see the only person for whom I have felt disinterested love, clutch at a shadow and read golden prophecies into the cautious utterances of a shoddy oracle." He devised a new numbering system to enable him to keep strict track of his and Edith's letters to each other, in an attempt to clarify their epistolary conversations and reduce the misunderstandings caused by the postal delays. She was to use Arabic numerals, and he Roman, so that they would know which letters they were replying to.

Ralph had been promoted to the rank of lance-corporal and was being moved about all over Britain for his military training. At least this gave him the opportunity to see parts of his country for the first time. Whilst he loved being in the mountains and by the sea, not all new experiences were welcome: he would always remember breakfasts in Barmouth when his landlady cooked bacon, which, as a Jew, he had never tasted and could not bring himself to eat. He decided to dispose of it discreetly. Another abiding memory of his time at Barmouth was the drill, and how on one occasion, the sergeant-major bellowing the orders 'left, right, left, right' made the soldiers march into the sea.

Although he found the physical training demanding, there was plenty of slack time when he might have enjoyed playing chess, except that there was no-one of his standard to play with. He complained to Edith about being the subordinate of a twenty-year-old ignoramus and about the 'coarse swearing, salacious anecdotes and desperate spinelessness' of his fellow soldiers. He and Johnny agreed about the maddening boredom induced by army routine. Johnny compared being in the R.A.F. to living in a monastery – although, granted, they used 'the salute instead of "Ave Maria" and they polished buttons and not the altar trappings'. In the same vein, Ralph told Edith that everyone was obsessed with the trivialities of everyday life, where the crease in one's trousers took on more importance than the advance of the

Germans in Russia. He hinted to her that once promoted, there was a chance that his work might bring them closer together: soon he would be given what he alluded to, vaguely, as 'a desk job'. Was he hoping that this would take him to France?

When Ralph returned to the flat in Hackney on leave, a wave of Russo-philia was sweeping over London in the form of Russian theatre, Russian ballet, Russian opera, Russian cinema and Russian music. He must have been infected by this enthusiasm for all things Russian. He started listening to Shostakovich, bought a copy of Dostoyevsky's *Crime and Punishment* and decided to teach himself the language using 78 rpm discs. He was still very interested in Freud, studying many of his works. Edith was quite at home with Freudian theories which had already gone out of fashion during her stay in Vienna, to be replaced by the ideas of other psychotherapists such as Adler and Erwin Wexberg. In her opinion, Freud focused much too much on sexual matters.

The vagueness in Edith's letters, alluded to by Ralph, was probably quite deliberate on her part. Not only did she not want to worry him, but she also felt it was self-indulgent to focus on her own problems when, as she put it, 'the rest of the world was in flames'. She told him that she had little to report about her life, which was solitary and monotonous. When Reinhold sold his car, the family had some money to fall back on, although, of course, this would not last long. Eventually, after giving a charity concert, Edith had attracted some pupils who paid just about enough to enable her to make ends meet. Although she did not enjoy piano teaching much, especially when the pupils asked to learn jazz and swing music, she thought she was getting better at it. She also gave private tuition to a young girl on the school curriculum. She reported that the winter had been very hard; many a time heavy snowfall had cut the family off from the outside world but with the coming of spring, everything seemed a bit better. In response to this letter, Ralph attempted to arrange to send Edith small sums of money, only to find that this was against the regulations.

Despite her attempts at optimism, Edith's bitterness and disillusion with humanity seep through her letters. She found people egoistic and indifferent to anything which did not affect them directly; they were all too ready to latch on to chimaeras and to swallow political slogans. Some people, whom she had thought of as friends, had distanced themselves from her. Scattered in her letters are cryptic comments about people 'wasting time and cheating'. There is the sense that she was struggling both physically and psychologically to maintain her equilibrium and to hold on to the hope she had for a better future, whilst dealing with the painful anxiety about her parents' safety. As ever, she clung to the two most important things in her life: her love for Ralph and her music. Listening to music on French radio, she told Ralph, was 'a good substitute for fresh food', and she was overjoyed, when, out of the blue one day, she received the entire library of sheet music she had left behind in Paris. She set herself the arduous task of mastering Schumann's *Études Symphoniques*, a piece of very great technical difficulty which reputedly caused Schumann to permanently injure one of his hands, ruining his prospects of a career as a pianist.

It was now three years since their last meeting. They felt they were ageing and changing – after all they were both approaching thirty! Their idyll in Paris together was fading into what seemed like a dream. For Edith, this served as an internal anchor, but Ralph's reaction was not the same: she was most upset when she read his comment that, "life continues, and time passes, passes without us getting any nearer to each other – let's hope it does not distance us", and again in a subsequent letter, more bluntly, "fatally we are growing further apart with each day that passes. Do I have to repeat that I need your lovely presence, but I am also afraid, terribly afraid of being disappointed?"

Again, he fell back on material concerns as obstacles to their marriage, telling her about "all these things I want you to have and to which you have a right – a suitable flat, big enough for our parallel lives to cross without bumping into each other, pretty dresses, a grand piano – will I be able to provide them?" Interestingly, this vision of their future 'parallel lives' together was to prove quite accurate. Naturally Edith felt hurt when she received letters like this. Every time he talked about feeling more distant, it was as if he had delivered her a blow, and she admitted that sometimes she feared that he might have found someone else. He replied that he respected her far too much to deceive her – 'at least in that way'. A slender figure and a pretty face might make him turn round but it did not turn his head. At times, she confessed, the hardship and isolation drained her energies, but she usually rallied; simply bringing him to mind gave her 'sweet consolation'. She wanted to explain what she was feeling for him when she signed off 'with all my tenderness': it meant her 'very great confidence in what he wanted to do in life', her admiration for his humanitarian ideas and the abandonment of herself to him.

Ralph's messages were mixed: discouragingly, he warned her that she should learn to envisage a future without him, since, as a soldier, there was always a chance that he might be killed in action. On the other hand, he reassured her about his intentions: "Let's look at the worst scenario; suppose your worst fears are confirmed and I don't love you any more – even if that were the case, I would do *everything* to rescue you from the restricted life you are leading. But that is not the case. I don't imagine my future without you." Most significantly, he shared the news that Esther, whom he alluded to as his 'best friend's wife', was about to have a baby, adding, "Please God it will be my turn one day".

Ralph's coolness prompted Edith to throw herself into her world of music with renewed tenacity and fervour. In the summer of 1942, she took the opportunity of meeting the other idol in her life, her teacher, Yvonne Lefébure, who was staying in Marseilles. Edith may well have travelled there from Bussières with Reinhold and Annie, on their way to their clandestine and blighted mission. Even Reinhold, she told Ralph, whose outlook was 'relentlessly materialistic', and who generally held music to be 'the most useless of pursuits', had understood that Edith was better protected against uncertainty and catastrophe than most people, thanks to her art.

The meeting with Yvonne (including four long lessons for which she refused any payment) was very intense, making a profound impression on Edith, which she described at length in a letter to Ralph. She was exhilarated by Yvonne's performance of *Children's Corner* by Debussy which had recently been played on the radio. Exchanging their deepest thoughts and feelings during the lessons, the two women discussed love and religion in relation to their music. Yvonne was sure that God existed: how else could one explain the genius of Beethoven?

Afterwards, Edith felt both inspired and demoralised: although Yvonne had told her that she had made enormous progress, Edith felt that she would never be able to emulate her. She had been thinking of herself as an artist but, as she confessed to Ralph, "Mlle Lefébure showed me how great Art is and how small I am." Returning to her room in a state of collapse and despondency, she resolved to close the piano for ever because 'it would never give up its secrets' to her. After resting, she went out for an evening walk up the hill to the famous basilica of Notre Dame de la Garde, where she found herself all alone, in a strong, warm breeze, gazing at the sun setting over the sea, dazzling and sparkling with "a thousand nuances. As far as the eye could see, there was sea and sky, sea and sky, and the rays of the sun". An overwhelming, unforgettable sense of infinite grandeur and her own humility swept over her. Suddenly, she felt the same way about Art as she was feeling about Nature. In a moment of transcendence, she realised that all her life she would be striving towards perfection in her playing, knowing that she had no hope of achieving it.

This experience enabled Edith to articulate the philosophy which was to give her strength during her most difficult times. She learned to rely on what she called her 'inner resources', which resided in the deepest level of her being, even if Ralph caused her hurt and pain. She told him that the piano was her life. "What would become of me without my music? My life would be terrible! ...You say you need a *raison d'être*, yes, true, but this *raison d'être* must be within you. We possess nothing other than what is within us. Everything else is an illusion and a harmful one."

*

It was just at this time, July 1942, when large numbers of Jews were deported to Auschwitz from Drancy in Paris; by August, the Vichy government was also starting to round up and deport Jews from the 'Free Zone'. Their priority was to get rid of foreign nationals, which, of course, included the Kern family. Reinhold, under the cover of his banal day job as bookkeeper for the local silk weaving enterprise, was becoming more deeply involved in the local resistance movement, *Libération-Sud*. He also charged himself with assuring the safety of his own family, Fa, Edith and Annie. Initially his remit for the resistance movement was in propaganda and recruitment. Dr Daniel Eyraud, his highly regarded colleague, was also a member of the movement, as was the parish priest, but there was little other support for the Resistance from people he knew in the community. Reinhold noted in his autobiography, *Mes quatre vies*, that the local bourgeoisie, amongst whom he had had so many friends before the war, were against the Allies and that most people in that circle seemed impervious to the seriousness of political events, since they were not directly affected. All this made it difficult to attract new recruits.

Since he had been obliged to sell his car, the delivery of propaganda leaflets took Reinhold on extended bicycle rides all over the countryside. He recorded that on many a Sunday, he did a round trip of one hundred and fifty kilometres! Here, the relationships he had established with patients during his years as the local doctor stood him in very good stead. He was impressed with the willingness of ordinary people to help and support the movement, especially the peasant farmers who had mostly been veterans of the First World War.

By the end of 1942, Reinhold had risen in *Libération-Sud*, becoming a member of its executive committee. He was put in charge of paramilitary operations for the whole *Département* of the Loire. This entailed planning for an armed rebellion, hiding weapons, planning street fighting, deciding where to place barricades, and selecting the first buildings to be occupied should there be a coup d'état. He also reconnoitred fields to assess their suitability as secret landing places for aeroplanes and parachutes bearing men and weapons. Unbeknown to his boss, Monsieur Mollon at the weaving factory, Reinhold used his place of work to store all his secret documents. When, after the war, Reinhold confessed everything to him poor Monsieur Mollon nearly had a fit.

Resistance work, highly risky at the best of times, had become even more dangerous. Many members of the network were discovered and executed, and later the leader of the movement, Jean Moulin, was captured by the Gestapo and tortured to death. Reinhold was working closely with a certain Monsieur Fernand Bonis in St Etienne, an electrician by training, who was assigned to receive signals in Morse code from de Gaulle's forces in London. On Christmas Eve of 1942, Reinhold received a phone call advising him to 'disappear' as fast as possible. Monsieur Bonis had just been caught and three other Resistance members had been arrested. He fled to the countryside, hiding about ten kilometres away from home. Again, the contacts from his years as the local doctor proved invaluable. While there was no police service in Bussières itself, Reinhold was known and respected by members of the force in the neighbouring communities, who made sure he had some extra time in which to escape.

Having shared their lives since they were teenagers, Fa and Reinhold now had to say goodbye to each other and to Annie, not knowing if they would ever see each other again – surely one of the most difficult moments of their lives. They entrusted Annie to the care of a close friend and later to their staunch colleague, Dr Eyraud. Reinhold then went to Lyon, where he jettisoned his alias, 'Georges Leblond', and obtained new false papers. Fa followed him later and was given the identity of a young woman who had died. Their aim was to join General de Gaulle's forces in London.

It was also thanks to Reinhold's efforts to arrange for her to have false identity papers and a guide that Edith was able to flee from Bussières in the September of 1942. This was just in the nick of time. Only a few weeks later, the German army entered Vichy France in retaliation against the French for supporting the landing of Allied troops in North Africa. Bussières was approximately five hundred kilometres from the border; Edith's journey to Switzerland must have been long and complex. Much of it would have been by road, but the last part of it was on foot in the high Alps. According to the *New York Times* correspondent in Berne at the time, there was a "continuous stream of Jewish refugees arriving from France". He continued, "they are in a sorry state. Many climbed to ten thousand feet in the Mont Blanc range to escape the French gendarmes. Some died en route".

Ralph first received the news that Edith had escaped from Reinhold, in a letter couched in coded language, where he implied that Edith's reason for going to Switzerland was for the benefit of her health: "No doubt the air will do her good. She wanted to be in good health ready for the time when she can be reunited with you." Reading between the lines, the separation of brother and sister had been painful for them both. Reinhold spoke of the great affection between him and Edith, implying that she would not have risked her life by fleeing if it had not been for her hope of a future with Ralph. Her courage and optimism would help her to endure whatever was in store. He was also at pains to explain indirectly to Ralph, who had been encouraging Edith to apply for an American visa so that she could stay with his uncle and aunt in Brooklyn, that this would have been too late. Otherwise 'everything was peaceful' at Bussières with life continuing 'as usual'. Reinhold undertook to forward Ralph's letters to Edith.

As Edith did not share many details with Ralph regarding her escape, we will never know exactly what happened. It was without doubt the most frightening experience of her life. Ralph received the following few lines, written in haste on a scrap of paper with no address, dated 8th October 1942. "My dear Ralph, I'm seizing this opportunity to write you a few words. As you must already know, I have arrived safely in Switzerland and I am relatively OK. If I had stayed, it is possible, even probable that we would never have seen each other again. At the moment I can't give you any details about my life. Find out if there is any possibility of my coming to you. I really don't know when I'll be able to write to you again. Write to Mme Welti, Palmstrasse 28. Write often. Your letters are the only connection I have with those who are dear to me and from whom I am now completely cut off. I am sure that my relations' home won't exist any longer in a short time. What can I add? Everything I have done I have done for you. I learned that love is a force capable of overcoming fatigue and danger. I came through, I preserved my virginity against all odds. I am more attached to you than all my family and my piano. We will meet again. I must finish. As you can guess, I am writing in great haste. If you believe in telepathy, you must have felt something of the flood of tenderness that went towards you recently. Edith."

What I do know of Edith's escape is what I can remember her telling me just before she died in 1972, when I was eighteen. I understood, at that time, that Edith felt that this episode had been one of the most defining experiences of her life, and that it was imperative for me to know about it. The guide, or *passeur*, to whose care she had been entrusted for the journey, had tried to rape her as they crossed the Alps on foot. Somehow, she had managed to wrench herself free and get away. The effort of running away, followed by arduous climbing and hiking, must have been enormous, particularly as Edith was not in the least bit sportive. It was a miracle that she managed the climb to reach the border in the high mountains. As she stepped into Switzerland, she was immediately overpowered by a huge tide of elation. The magnificent sight of mountain peaks rolling infinitely to the east, and the realisation that she was safe at last, suddenly released her from the intense stress of the previous few days, weeks and months. This experience of transcendence and religious joy was to sustain her for the rest of her life. When she tried to put it into words for me, she described it as akin to what she felt when listening to Beethoven's last piano sonatas – a state of visionary ecstasy which could only come from God.

This was the second time Edith had glimpsed the infinite, the first having been in Marseilles when she understood her place as an artist. I believe that these intense feelings resulted from the life of austerity, both material and psychological, that she had been leading for the preceding two years in Bussières, a life that was almost monastic in its privations, which might well have predisposed her to experience a revelation like those of the saints.

Although Ralph had been aware that Edith had been suffering great hardship, he was profoundly shocked when he realised the great danger she had undergone. Subsequently, she admitted that there had been much she had kept from him so as not to worry him unduly. Ralph wrote: "The letter from your brother and your two letters left me breathless with the revelations that filled me with anxiety. What a *coup de théâtre!*" For them both, Edith's traumatic escape from France brought their love into sharp focus. As Edith put it, "one cannot judge the true intensity of one's feelings except in the most serious moments of one's life, or through the ordeals such as I have just experienced." Overcome with emotion, Ralph replied: "No need to say how much I miss you. I need you so much more than you need me. I need your affection, of which I have been deprived all my life. I need your intelligence, your devotion and above all, your good will."

Edith was lucky not to have fallen victim to the *passeur*. Many of these guides or, to put it more accurately, 'people smugglers', belonged to the underworld of petty criminals, engaged in the illegal trafficking of gold and money across the borders. They were known to blackmail the people they were supposed to be helping, or worse still, rob them, abandon them, or even hand them over to the Gestapo once they had received payment. Yet refugees were forced to put themselves in the hands of the *passeurs* and hope for the best, because of their intimate knowledge of the terrain and the border.

The official rule of the Swiss government was to turn back Jews and any refugees without a visa. This policy had been hardening since 1933, when increasing numbers of people escaping the Nazis had attempted to seek asylum in Switzerland.

The government considered that retaining neutral status was essential for the survival of the small landlocked nation, even more so after the onset of war, surrounded as it was by German-occupied territory. They certainly knew that Jewish people who were refused entry would meet their death at the hands of the Gestapo, and it was widely known that by July 1942, the Nazis had killed around one million Jews. Thomas Mann had stated in a radio broadcast on 27th September 1942 that the Nazis' aim was 'the complete obliteration of European Jewry'.

Arguments to support the government policy – all too familiar today – were to do with the fear of being 'flooded by alien elements', the security risks of admitting refugees, and the lack of resources to feed and accommodate them. However, Swiss people rose up in anger against the government policy in a nation-wide protest supported by well-known personalities, forcing the government to back down and open the borders again. Once the anger of the people had died down, the government reinstated the policy of tightened border control. In recent years, it has come to light that Swiss banks were laundering money on behalf of the Nazis, money which had come from plundered gold and valuables.

In any case, the border zone, a broad strip of land twelve kilometres wide, was difficult to patrol. There must always have been 'porous' areas where it was not clearly marked and where it was unmanned. There were also many organisations of local people who were committed to helping Jews to safety, and several thousands were helped in this way. Edith probably arrived during the short window of time where the government was responding to public protest. What her movements were after setting foot on Swiss soil remains a mystery. She was presumably received for a few days at a pre-arranged place, but we neither know the location of 'Palmstrasse' or who Mme Welti was. From there, Edith might have taken a train to Berne, where she very quickly found work and accommodation in Montbijour Strasse 11, care of a Mme A. Schwob. All this we know from the delighted letter Edith received from her parents. Edith had reported that she was safe and happy, enjoying good food, teaching schoolchildren various subjects, including geography, for twenty-five hours per week and was even preparing a programme for a concert.

After expressing her relief, Martha was quick to revert to her usual concerns about Edith's wardrobe: did she have a nice concert dress? – and what about shoes? Whilst daily life was still difficult for them in Czernowitz, it had improved somewhat since Martha was now working all hours teaching private pupils at home. She pined for her children and had found an old jumper of 'Reini's' which she was wearing because it still carried his smell. Theodor, alias Dorothea, a great nature worshipper himself, was overjoyed that Edith was living in beautiful mountainous surroundings. However, all this proved to be a false dawn: after a few weeks of 'normality', Edith was transferred to the canton of Lucerne, where she was interned.

9

INTERNMENT

The beginning of 1943 saw the whole family scattered across Europe, with little sense of connection. Nobody could be sure of Edith's whereabouts in Switzerland, Reinhold was crossing the Pyrenees from France into Spain on foot, Fa was somewhere behind on her way to join him, Annie was still in France in the care of trusted friends, Martha, Theodor and grandmother Rosa were subsisting in Czernowitz, Annie's parents, Bina and Emo, were surviving the Łódź ghetto, while Ralph was sent to army bases that took him all over Britain on 'various commissions'.

It was a time of isolation and anxiety for Edith and Ralph. Postal services had been suspended between Britain and Switzerland since October 1942, not to be resumed until three months later at the end of January of 1943. When Ralph eventually received news from Edith, he was overcome at the sight of the envelope addressed in the dear handwriting – as abominable as ever – hardly daring to open the letter. What was inside, what could it reveal? Ralph looked hard between the lines for more information. So much had happened to Edith during the last few months, leaving so many questions unanswered.

Edith informed Ralph that since her arrival in Switzerland, she had moved three times and was now living in a hotel in Kriens, near Luzern, in the centre of the country, where she expected she would be staying for some time. She had managed to send Ralph a card postmarked from La Chaux-de-Fonds, a small town in the Jura Mountains near the border, renowned as an important centre of Swiss watchmaking. How she had reached the border and what her subsequent movements had been remained unexplained. The only detail she had mentioned was that she had had to sleep on a dormitory floor.

However, the Swiss National Archive has preserved Edith's refugee file, running, astonishingly, to over seventy documents, consisting mostly of a plethora of police forms. Amongst these is a record of her route. It transpires that she had left Bussières on September 15th 1942, following a route via Lyon, Evian, then across the mountains to the border at Thollen, and onwards to St Gingolf, intending to reach Berne. St Gingolf was a well-known spot for smuggling arms and Jews. A border guard at St Gingolf recorded that on Sunday 27th September at 5pm, he arrested a young Romanian Jew by the name of Edith Kern. After repeated interrogations, Edith was interned in three separate camps before arriving at the work camp in December 1942, where she was to remain for a year.

What is still not clear is how she managed to work in Berne before she was interned. The three camps (first Martigny, then Bex for five weeks and finally one situated in a small village called Münchwilen) were none of them too far from Berne, so it is conceivable that she commuted to her work as a teacher in that city. What is more difficult to understand is why the authorities permitted her to do it. During those two short months in Berne, Edith had rapidly made a new life for herself, making several friends in the world of music, and even performing in public, in addition to securing employment as

Ralph's grandfather, Dov Behr Lubotsky

Ralph's mother, Jane

Edith's parents, Martha and Theodor, on a mountain walk

Edith aged about 3

Bernie (left) and Ralph (right) in outfits made by their mother

Edith aged 23

Ralph aged 23

Bernie in uniform

Reinhold, Fa and Ralph in uniform

Annie with Fa and Reinhold

Edith and Ralph on their wedding day

Reinhold's forged permit to enter the Soviet Union

Edith's mother, Martha, before the war   *Edith's mother, Martha, just after the war*

Ralph's father, Alec and his sister, Rivka Leah

Edith and Ralph in the drawing room at Porson Road

Ralph in his study at Trinity

a schoolteacher. All this ended abruptly, presumably when she was identified as a refugee by the authorities, since it was illegal to employ foreigners without a visa. She would then have been granted a 'tolerance permit' enabling her to stay in the country and sent to 'Sonnenberg', Kriens.

Sonnenberg Hotel had been disused for many years prior to the war. At one time, it had been one of the largest rest cure establishments in the country. Situated in a spot of outstanding beauty, just above the small town of Kriens, from which it could be reached by funicular, the hotel had been an ideal location for holidays and recuperation. In December 1942 it was reopened as an internment hostel for up to two hundred women. By all accounts, it was a sad place. Women with husbands and children were separated from their loved ones, who were sent to other parts of the country and whom they were only occasionally allowed to visit. Isolation was one of the aims of the national policy, since it was considered undesirable for refugees to mix with the local population; there had been hostility from some groups in society towards the steady flow of immigrants to Switzerland fleeing from the Nazi regime since 1933. Edith was desperately unhappy; cut off from Ralph and her family, feeling totally alone, she struggled with despair in her 'gilded cage'. How she would have liked to send Ralph birthday wishes for the sixth of January but could only hope that telepathy might work instead.

Initially, she was placed in a room with three other women. From her window there was a view of the lake below, surrounded by the forested, snow-capped mountains of Rigi and Pilatus enveloped in a 'sea of fairy-tale clouds'. She only wished Ralph could also have enjoyed the magnificent sight of the forest in all shades of green, and the reflection of the mountains in the calm water changing colour every hour – a magical scene, especially at sunset. Edith had no complaints about comfort or food, which was simple and plentiful, albeit relying heavily on the potato. The ethos was one of discipline enforced by a rigid timetable. The women were required to work in silence without exchanging a word, and those whose efforts were deemed satisfactory were granted more leave. Edith's duties included polishing the parquet floor, cleaning the windows, emptying bins and fetching wood – intensely frustrating after her interlude of fulfilment, teaching and performing in Berne. Later she was required to knit socks which she enjoyed, although she was not allowed to knit anything for Ralph.

When Ralph asked for more details about her daily life, she provided him with a fuller report, all in the third person as if to emphasise her sense of alienation. She told him that "Edith was adapting quite well to her new way of life, performing all her tasks philosophically, finding no job beneath her". She described the intense monitoring of all the inmates' activities: the young women were only allowed out of the hostel during the week and only during the day at that. The building was generally locked, except for a short period at lunchtime, when they were made to walk in a line in a small area outside. Every change of activity in the timetable of housework was signalled by the clang of a large cowbell, which in total was sounded eleven times each day, starting at 6.30 in the morning when it was time to get up. Bedtime and lights out were strictly at 10pm.

One of the most trying aspects of life was the twice-daily roll call, conducted by the Director. This, more than anything else, brought home to Edith her status as a prisoner. It gave the Director the opportunity to remind the women of the rules of the establishment, to make accusations and admonishments for infringements, and to lay down further restrictions. Edith tried hard to focus on her sense of inner freedom, not daring to think about the end of the war or being reunited with the people she loved. During these initial few weeks, she was also trying to recover from the trauma of her escape from France. When Ralph asked her if she was still wearing a certain dress, a favourite of his, she reminded him that she had jettisoned her rucksack and all its contents when getting away from the man who had tried to rape her, adding that what she had managed to preserve was worth any number of dresses.

*

Ralph also continued to be dissatisfied and frustrated with army life. He longed for a more stimulating role, and to be making a more useful contribution to the war effort. "Intellectuals, according to Stendhal, need to devour a certain quantity of cubic metres of ideas per day," he told Edith. He continued to suffer from a feeling of inner emptiness which only she could fill; as ever, he complained that he lacked a *raison d'être*. Rather Britishly, he said he 'mustn't grumble' since what she was going through was far worse – however, grumble he would because he had nothing better to do! Nevertheless, with regular pay from the army, he was now feeling more relaxed about his financial situation and had become very preoccupied with the prospect of marriage.

*

Whilst Ralph and Edith were whiling away time feeling trapped and frustrated, Reinhold was tramping across the Pyrenees in a group organised by the Resistance. This proved to be a lengthy and hazardous journey, punctuated with moments of terror. Young and fit, Reinhold coped well with the arduous ascents and descents in snow so deep that it sometimes reached his hips. There was an older and less robust member of the party who would not have survived without the help of Reinhold and another man who carried him up the mountain for one leg of the journey. Nominated leader of the group, Reinhold decided to take the risk of descending to the valley where the walking was easier, after they had all spent a night in a semi-frozen state in an abandoned mountain cabin. Although this was more dangerous because it was more exposed, he was sure that otherwise his colleague would never have survived the cold and exhaustion higher up.

The group made their descent on New Year's Eve of 1942, having, during one terrible moment, to lie flat and hold their breath in the forest, as two patrolling German soldiers walked by. Eventually, they arrived in a Spanish village, where they had the choice of turning themselves in and being imprisoned, or continuing further, walking the not inconsiderable distance to neutral Portugal. At this point they struck lucky. Some lumberjacks, who had fought against Franco, took them under their wing, enabling them to recuperate for a couple of days before taking them by river towards Portugal. After walking for a further two days, they found themselves running out of food and were forced to send a member of the group into a village to buy bread. This proved to be their undoing: the baker immediately informed the authorities, whereupon they were arrested and taken to prison in Pamplona.

Reinhold wrote in his autobiography that he found the two months he spent in prison in Pamplona an 'interesting and enriching' experience. This was thanks to the six people with whom he shared a cell meant for two. He and his cell mates soon created a routine for themselves which enabled them to maintain their dignity and cleanliness, whilst entertaining each other to pass the time. During his imprisonment, Reinhold lost twelve kilogrammes on the twice-daily diet of bread and soup. It was only by the end of March that Edith received the news from Reinhold in a card from Pamplona prison signed 'Ernest Quairne', that he had managed to cross the border into

Spain. Weekly postcards from her parents from Czernowitz were getting through, including special birthday wishes for the seventeenth of February from her grandmother, now aged eighty-four.

*

Life was gradually getting a little easier in Czernowitz: Martha reported that they were eating better, although there were still no desserts, and Papa, with his sweet tooth, was suffering from having to make do with nuts instead. She was now eking out a living by teaching all hours, including Saturdays. In the evenings she devoted herself to darning and sewing and had recently overhauled Edith's wardrobe. "How is your laundry?" she asked her daughter. "How I wish I could help you with it…" Martha had friends in Switzerland with whom she encouraged Edith to make contact, especially Ninon Hesse, who was living in Davos.

Edith's parents and grandmother were generally recovering from the traumatic events of 1941, only Martha's hair was now 'more silver than gold'. A semblance of normal life was resuming. Friends were coming to the flat to play bridge as before, but Grandmother was having to bring Martha soothing valerian infusions at night to calm her nerves and help her sleep. They had heard nothing from Fa's parents. Since attempts to trace them had led nowhere, they must have suspected that they had died at the hands of the Nazis. Indeed, it later transpired that they were shot sometime in 1942 after deportation to Transnistria. Martha was pining for her children, confessing to Edith, "I have sometimes such unbelievable longing for you that it gives me physical pain."

*

Edith's state of 'unbearable uncertainty' ended in a flood of relief when postal services between Switzerland and Britain were reopened, and she finally heard from Ralph. However, although eagerly awaited, his letters often made her sad because she was forming the inevitable impression that for him, she was 'sliding into the past'. He told her that increasingly, he perceived her as a 'mythological, almost imaginary creature' representing Paris, a period of happiness so distant as to feel unreal. At this time, Ralph was rereading *À la recherche du temps perdu* by Proust, which seemed to influence the way he wrote of the past in his correspondence with Edith. They reminisced again about their strolls together under the pink-flowering chestnut trees of Boulevard Arago back in 1939, the outings they had to cafés, restaurants and the opera (when on one occasion, Edith, to her embarrassment, had fallen asleep), reliving the happiness of their brief, carefree time together, thereby attempting to prevent its eclipse by the subsequent years of war and separation. The psychology of Proust may have been of special interest to Ralph as a homosexual; he commented in a letter to Edith that he sensed that Proust did not like women – not one of his female characters was intelligent or good-natured.

It was during 1943 that Edith and Ralph confronted the underlying problems in their relationship. Edith was no longer satisfied with leaving major issues unexplored. She decided she must grasp an important nettle and told him that she did not accept his view that it was 'the perversity of destiny' that had prevented their union, leading to their separation. No, during the last four years, there had been 'a thousand missed opportunities'. It was not financial problems or the difficulties of travel that had been the barrier, but rather something *within* Ralph that had always caused him to step back from the ultimate commitment. And now he was still talking about her obtaining a visa to get to America! Didn't he realise that now more than ever before she could do *nothing* for herself? "What," she continued, "could have prevented you from coming to me completely? I don't know, perhaps I can guess, but I do not want to know more than what you feel you can confide… I just want to address a prayer to you. This thing that keeps you from me and makes you tense, couldn't you overcome it? Don't you realise that whatever you say and whatever you do, that I would understand? Isn't it a big source of security to allow yourself to repose in such great love as mine for you? *Je t'embrasse mon grand chéri.* In future, dare to impose on me whatever you need to. I will never betray your trust. I am not a feeble reed. I can bear a lot and I want you to tell me what you think."

How could Ralph avoid responding to this letter? He could not help but be touched by her candour and trust, moved by her calm, dignity and purity. In a letter that he never sent he replied, "Yes, I will speak, because you have asked me to do so, with all the frankness I am capable of. Oedipus asked to know things which did not contribute much to his happiness. Let's hope that in your case you have the strength to bear the heavy weight of the truth you demand, because you are right and more so than you think." There followed in this unsent letter, some cruel words: "In Paris you loved me. I did not love you. I found you gifted and charming. We were good friends and I liked you – that was all." He then explained that he had been going through a crisis of unrequited love, although he did not mention that the object of his love was a man, Henry Rudolf. But then things changed. Once back in London, Ralph started to miss Edith, realising how much she had meant to him. He was also aware of her love for him and feared hurting her, expecting that she would forget him in time, even rather hoping this would happen since he felt so unworthy of her. "That was what I was thinking consciously. But at the same time, there was an unarticulated unconscious gestation. The war, the fall of Paris, the thought that with all the will in the world I could not see you anymore, or hear your voice, or hear you play the piano brought these feelings to the surface. I felt that if I didn't share my life with you, that it could never be with any other woman. And now I felt more bound to you than ever. The idea of being with another woman (and you can well imagine I have had opportunities in the last four years) is grotesque. But is this love? I am without passion. If it is love, I am not in love. But there are many ways of loving – the test will be in sharing our lives. I have been madly in love with all my being with no return. It nearly destroyed me. Something now in me has died forever... I didn't want to tell you this before we met again, when face to face, I would have told you and other things... I am suppressing tears now because I am not the sort of person who cries with self-pity. I had a treatment, I am better, but not cured – I will also have to explain to you face to face."

It is clear from this letter that Ralph fully intended to discuss his homosexuality with Edith when they met again after the war and entirely understandable that he did not want to spell this out in a letter at a time when their correspondence was more closely scrutinised by the censors than ever. Each page of each letter at this stage of the war was marked by a diagonal blue stripe and the envelopes were studded with examiners' numbers from both England and Germany stating, 'Opened examiner xxxxx' and 'Geöffnet Oberkommando der Wehrmacht' with the Third Reich's stamp of the eagle and swastika. Clearly Ralph had far too much to lose from revealing his homosexuality. However, the mere act of writing down his feelings in the unsent letter may have been therapeutic.

There was another important matter which Ralph and Edith needed to thrash out: Ralph was making his desire to have a family with Edith abundantly clear, without suspecting that she was completely against it. One of the main reasons for wanting to have children – his fantasy was to have a family of six – was to 'wash away the sins of the present generation for having allowed this war, this crime against humanity'. He resented the time passing, when they might have been seeing their children growing up.

Edith felt she owed him the truth regarding her views on the subject of children; attempting to settle the matter, she wrote, "Please allow me to clarify one thing: children. If I don't want to have children, it's because I do not want to perpetuate suffering to which any child of mine would be exposed." Ralph was furious when he received this letter, replying, "So you have decided 'firmly and irrevocably' not to have children have you? But wait a minute. I don't intend to travel to Berchtesgaden[12] on my honeymoon! When discussing my future, my aspirations and anything that concerns me, I expect to have a right of reply and have my voice heard!" What if he told her that it was his 'firm and irrevocable decision' to have ten children? He demanded to know her reasons for such an unnatural choice, adding bitingly that of course he had forgotten his role, which was to be responsible for everything: "reading your letters one would think it was me who caused the war!"

The war had given Edith a pessimistic outlook on the future: 'One can't change human nature.' Whenever she heard that there would be no more wars after this one, she had to smile. "Men have been fighting wars for more than seven thousand years and there is no reason why this should stop. Jealousy, greed, revenge and covetousness will always remain at the bottom of the human soul, which no war, no victory on whatever scale can extinguish. You must understand that it is not a lack of love but rather an excess of it which makes me feel like this. I shudder to think that a poor, innocent creature might have to undergo what I went through." Edith felt so strongly about it that she was even prepared to consider an end to their relationship if they could not reach agreement. "I love you much too much to want to bar you from fulfilment and happiness. Think about it. You know, I will never be lost as long as I have my piano."

Both Edith and Ralph were shaken by this storm in their correspondence. Edith was unable to eat or sleep, feeling utterly forlorn amongst the indifferent strangers in the hostel. She told Ralph that she wanted to draw a line under all their disagreements and never wanted to argue with him again, expressing again the depth of her feeling for him: "I will think of you now I am going to sleep, and your image will cross with me through the door of consciousness and will accompany me to a deeper region where only you can enter." Making light of the issue, Ralph asked to have the last word: "You tell me that there are invisible bonds (*fils* in French) which pass between us – but I would prefer the visible kinds of *fils* (sons), which are called, 'Jean-Pierre', 'Charles-Phillipe', 'François-Marie', etc." He knew that he needed her love. "Exiled and deprived of everything as you are, you are still richer than me. Carry on giving, because without your generosity, I am at risk of going under."

Edith gradually began to adapt to her new life as an internee. The arrival of spring brought hope, along with repeated German defeats, notably at the battle of Stalingrad. She was given permission to buy a piano and move it into her room, which she was now sharing with one other woman. She wrote to Ralph that 'the piano was looking at her in a friendly way, although it was just an old honkytonk which had been used for bashing out jazz' – at least it would help her maintain her technique. She was now making the most of opportunities to travel in Switzerland on her days off, having been up Mount Rigi and enjoyed the view which stretched as far as Lake Geneva. She had also been invited to fashionable Davos several times, visiting some of the places mentioned in *The Magic Mountain* by Thomas Mann, although she did not mention her mother's friend Ninon Hesse. Once the weather warmed up, she was looking forward to bathing in Lake Luzern, provided it was not too expensive. Following a performance in the hostel, which was enjoyed by some influential people, she was allocated a spare room to use as a studio for her piano practice, and the authorities let her off work every afternoon to do so. She was delighted when she was asked to work in a library, and the director was so pleased with her that he soon released her from all her chores in the hostel. Her days were now busy with practising and the library.

In Edith's file from the Swiss Archives there are several letters requesting that Fräulein Kern be given leave to help a woman by the name of Irma Bacler, who was no longer able to manage all her own housework and gardening because she was looking after her elderly parents. Edith had to complete a questionnaire on her suitability for this work, to which the director of the internment hostel added some comments which were not wholly complimentary: "Our camp resident, Edith Kern, makes heavy weather of the work, although she is very willing. Character good and adaptable. Has bad eyesight and is feeble and impractical..." After further formalities had duly passed backwards and forwards from police departments, Edith was finally granted permission for temporary leave. It seems that the application to help Frau Bacler was a ruse cooked up by Edith's Swiss friends to enable her to pursue her musical vocation. Indeed, during that summer, Edith's career started to blossom. She went from strength to strength, renewing contact with musicians she had met in Berne, which led to more public performances in Zürich and Winterthur, as well as many piano pupils.

For the first time in several years, Edith was feeling hopeful and content, informing Ralph that she was being spoilt with opportunities by her Swiss friends, who were taking a keen interest in her music. She was about to go and stay in a superb villa in Zürich and had been invited to play in Davos. Her programmes of lecture-recitals were proving very successful. To think that when she first arrived in Switzerland, she didn't know anyone! She was pleased to be earning some money from her music, enough to enable her to think of buying a new blue silk dress with white spots which had caught her eye, after making do with second-hand clothes for so long.

It was with great joy that she received the news that Reinhold had reached London. Following his release from prison in Pamplona, he had spent a further two months interned in a camp in the province of Burgos in northern Spain, and finally was put on a bomber bound for London from Gibraltar. Fa had reached Madrid and was also on her way to London. The prospect of a meeting between her beloved brother and Ralph caused Edith much excitement and she hoped Ralph would be able to facilitate Fa's arrival in London.

*

In the spring of 1943, after many months of frustration and boredom, Ralph's military career also took an upward turn, when he began to be allocated much more interesting work than hitherto. There would no longer be any time for Proust. Although Ralph never talked about what this work involved, it is very likely that he used his foreign language skills. The testimonial from the head teacher at Maiden Erlegh suggests that this would have been an appropriate use of Ralph's abilities: "He speaks French with so good an accent that he can easily be mistaken for a French man. He also speaks German fluently with a good accent, but not up to the standard to deceive a native of that country." Ralph followed the advice on the inside cover of his soldier's service and pay book to the letter: Addressed to 'All Ranks', it issued the following warning: "*Remember* – Never discuss military, naval or air matters in public or with any stranger, no matter to what nationality he or she may belong. The enemy wants information about you, your unit, your destination. He will do his utmost to discover it. Keep him in the dark. Gossip on military subjects is highly dangerous to the country, whereas secrecy leads to success. *Be on your guard* and report any suspicious individual." Interestingly, his religion in his service book was stated to be 'C of E'.

Ralph was transferred to Hartsbourne Manor in Hertfordshire, where the Battle of Britain had been masterminded in 1940. Here he worked flat out, informing Edith that his days were filled with feverish activity, when he only put down his pen and caught his breath at bedtime, unless he was on a mission which took him to the centre of the country. The most he told her about his work was that he now felt closely involved in the national war effort. His letters frequently included expressions of optimism that the war would shortly end in victory for the Allies. His sanguine attitude indicates that he had inside knowledge.

Despite being so busy, Ralph made the time to visit his father in Hackney, now sixty-five years old, living on his own and missing his other son, Bernie, who was on active service and had recently been promoted from private to lance-corporal. Ralph lamented that his father's ideas were becoming rigid with age, and that all his opinions were coloured by the First World War.

Edith and Ralph's thoughts were now tending towards a future they were going to share, instead of dwelling on the past. Ralph described a dream he had had of their buying a cottage on the River Loire together. He wanted to travel and explore the world. Edith replied that she would be happy to leave the decor of the cottage up to him, since he had far better taste. She was not interested in travel; all she wanted was a country and a home. Her most cherished dream was to be greeted from the train by Ralph and Reinhold waiting for her on the platform.

It was as if, having aired their disagreements, Edith and Ralph were thinking as a couple. Ralph's letters seemed to become more natural, although he did not hold back from expressing his fears about his 'condition' which would be bound to cause her a lot of pain and sadness. He was so looking forward to seeing her again and to giving her some consolation for her years of misfortune. He only hoped he would be up to the task. Above all, he did not want her to say one day that he had deceived her. "That's why you must learn to see me as I am and not how you would like me to be."

Soon Reinhold and Fa met Ralph in London and found they got on well. The two families were beginning to unite. Martha was with them all in spirit, writing to Edith, "You will laugh, but I have also dreamt about Ralph several times and warmly embraced him. I could be such a good mother to him."

In November 1943, Edith sat and passed the entrance examination to the Berne Conservatoire during one of her official short breaks from internment. She threw herself into preparation for a concert of Chopin's *Piano concerto in E minor* and the *Variations Symphoniques* by César Franck. Ralph was confident that he would soon be able to collect her. "How I would like to see you in that dress with blue and white spots – how I would love above all to hear you play." He would even swallow the lecture that went before the recital.

10

DENOUEMENT

The year 1944 was one of anticipation for Edith and Ralph, who were now both confident that the war would end in victory for the Allies and that they would meet again and marry as soon as possible. Already five years had passed since they had last seen each other, and they were no longer in their first flush of youth. In January Ralph reached his twenty-ninth birthday and in February Edith turned thirty. They were both desperate for this limbo to end; while Edith yearned for Ralph and the security of a home, Ralph's longing was mixed with apprehension.

In December of 1943, Edith was dealt a severe blow when she received the terrible news from Reinhold that their father, Theodor, had died in Czernowitz six months previously. Her mother, Reinhold, Fa and Ralph had all conspired to keep this from Edith at the time, because they considered that, all alone and interned in a foreign country, it would have been too distressing for her. Her one comfort was that her father had not suffered. He went to bed one night, after eating his favourite dessert of sour cherry compote, and died in his sleep of a heart attack. Several months previously he had been diagnosed with

131

cancer of the throat and might otherwise have had a lingering decline and death.

Edith plummeted into a state of deep mourning for a period of several months. Her bereavement coincided with the news that she was to be temporarily released from internment at the labour camp in Sonnenberg. Negotiations had started several months previously regarding Edith's further studies once she had managed to pass the entrance examination to the Berne Conservatoire. After protracted arrangements involving multiple form filling, supplemented by testimonials sent between the cantons of Berne and Luzern, she was finally allowed to enter the Conservatoire to study for the Concert Diploma for three months. In a supporting letter, her boss from the library vouched for Edith's 'polite and modest character' and her genuine love of music, adding that she had little aptitude or interest in practical work of any kind. The Reform Church at Winterthur guaranteed that it would meet the cost of Edith's classes during the semester, and a small grant for subsistence was provided by a Swiss charity. Without extra top-ups up from Reinhold, presumably via his network of contacts, she could not have managed and she looked up to him with gratitude as 'the brother of all brothers'.

During Edith's time in Berne, she was expected to report to the police every Wednesday and was not allowed out between the hours of 10pm and 7am. She was, naturally, completely indifferent to the rule forbidding her to frequent bars, dances or casinos, or to go out in a group of more than five people. She also had to sign a declaration that she would not earn any money, and that she would do her utmost to leave Switzerland as soon as possible. Whilst she did not mention any of these conditions in her letters to Ralph, she did admit to her dread of re-internment in April after finishing her studies. The previous year spent in detention had been a 'nightmare' and she would give anything not to have to go back to Sonnenberg.

On her thirtieth birthday she was lonely and sad, but Ralph's letter in which he assured her that this would be her last birthday all alone in a foreign land was of some comfort. Edith's sombre mood on resuming her studies improved greatly when she was able to devote herself to her piano once more. Her new teacher at the Conservatoire, Joseph Hirt, was clearly impressed with her playing, giving her much needed encouragement. She immersed herself in Schumann's piano concerto, which she found enthralling, and asked Ralph to compile a programme chosen from his favourite pieces for her to perform. She must have had rather a difficult time in Berne, as she was constantly obliged to move lodgings, piano and all, which was both costly and unsettling. Ralph attempted to send her extra money, only to find that it was against the regulations. She wondered about trying to earn some extra cash by playing in a café, even though that too was forbidden. Ralph thought it a good idea, reminding her that even Wagner had resorted to this when he was living in Paris.

In March she received some good news from Ralph: he had just been promoted to the rank of captain. He was now confident that the war was reaching its final stages and was optimistic that they would be able to meet again before the end of the year, once the campaign in Italy had been won by the Allies. Their main topic of discussion at this point was their future life together. Each expressed their support for the other's career: as Edith said to Ralph, "I know you have ambition and I will do everything to encourage you." Ralph was already thinking about how Edith could establish herself as a concert pianist before an English public: she should make sure she kept all newspaper cuttings of reviews in Switzerland and it was imperative that she continued working on her English – how else would she manage the vegetable shopping?

For the first time, Ralph's letters took on a romantic tone, which Edith found 'infinitely touching'. How she cherished the dried-up sprig of honeysuckle he had plucked for her from a hedgerow in Hertfordshire on his daily walk to work. She declared that 'she was not worthy of this attentiveness.' Ralph had by now adopted the style one would expect from a more conventional lover: he told her that if she closed her eyes, she would feel his kiss on her lips as he kissed her photograph. Yet, there was also a note of apprehension in Ralph's letters, a fear of being unworthy of her. "I know I don't deserve your love. When you get to know me better, I am afraid you will be greatly disappointed." He could give way to moments of gloom. "Life is not pleasant when the present is awful, the future frightening and the past nostalgic." Sometimes his vision of the future was gratuitously jaundiced. "You must not think that the end of the war will be the end of our worries – it will be the beginning of life, but life is just an uninterrupted series of problems."

Ralph continued to be stationed at Hartsbourne Manor in Hertfordshire, where it seems he had a tranquil time. His letters express delight as he registered the changing seasons in the countryside around him. He may well have taken part in the masterminding of Operation Overlord, the strategy for the Normandy invasions, planned to take place in June. Since this had already been completed by March, he evidently had a lot of time on his hands – time to read extensively (he mentions Goethe, Gibbon and Stendhal), visit the British Museum Library every week to continue his research on Jean-Jacques Rousseau, and to make another foolhardy attempt to learn Russian. Once again, he returned to the piano. Whilst in London, he browsed in the antiquarian book shops. It was at this period that he bought the first bargains of what was to become his magnificent library of eighteenth-century works.

Ralph spent the weekends with his father in the flat in Hackney. He resolved that he and Edith would not start their married life living there with his relatives. Clearly, he found the family flat embarrassing and rather shameful. To his father's chagrin, Ralph always kept his suitcase in the hall, as if he was an outsider with no intention of lingering any longer than necessary. He felt it was really his father's and Bernie's territory. In a letter (the writing of which was interrupted by a bomb alert) he gave Edith a detailed description of the flat. Although relatively modern, having been built in 1925, it was without a lift, heating or hot water. Smells of 'not very successful masculine cooking' wafted down the entrance passage. The living-room carpet was a distasteful shade of beige, showing up 'all the accumulated stains of four years of negligence and domestic disasters'. Whilst total chaos reigned in the room shared by Alec and Bernie, Ralph's room was perfectly neat and tidy. One redeeming feature, as far as he was concerned, was the view of the chestnut trees from the large window in the living room, a reminder of Paris.

Edith was delighted to learn that Ralph was seeing a lot of Reinhold and Fa since their arrival in London, and that he had even introduced them to his father and to Bernie when he came home on leave. To her great joy, she received the longed-for photograph of Ralph and another one of him with Reinhold and Fa, all in uniform. It had been so long since she had seen him that she could hardly remember what he looked like.

During the summer of 1944, the correspondence between Edith and Ralph was very patchy. This was partly because letters were suspended from England for three months from the time of the D-Day landings, and also because Edith moved so many times when she was living in Berne. Ralph complained that Edith's rare letters were becoming 'rarissimo', asking that she send him the occasional telegram to reassure him that all was well, only to grumble, when he did receive them, that the telegrams were unintelligible because they were devoid of punctuation. Sometimes the censor (whom Ralph had nicknamed 'Friedl') was over-zealous with the scissors: in one letter there was a big hole where there had been a passage of music. Presumably the censor had taken this to be a dangerous code of some sort. Letters from Edith were so infrequent that Ralph started to suspect that her affections had been stolen by Herr Hirt at the Conservatoire. "I need you so much and need to know that I am loved. What would I do without you?" Edith was quick to reassure him that Herr Hirt was just her teacher and could never be anything more for her.

The latter part of 1944 was very fulfilling for Edith. Happily, she was granted permission to continue her studies in Berne. She began to shine in her public performances, receiving many accolades, including very gratifying reviews in the newspapers. Her performance of Chopin, Debussy and Ravel was praised as 'virtuosic and intelligent'. She told Ralph that this had been the most productive year of her life. The pinnacle was probably when she played in the *Variations Symphoniques* by César Franck as the soloist with an orchestra for the first time, no mean achievement, as, in addition to the pianistic challenges, Edith was suffering from an abscess on her foot which needed incising and draining. The show had to go on despite doctor's orders because Herr Hirt had insisted on it. However, for all her musical success, Edith was still preoccupied with worry about her mother and how she was coping with life in Czernowitz without her father.

*

MARTHA AND ROSA IN CZERNOWITZ

By spring, the Soviet Army was advancing steadily through northern Bukovina, forcing the Germans to retreat. This situation made life more dangerous for the Jews, who were subjected to intensified persecution from the losing side. At the same time, many thousands of frightened Romanians who had stayed during the previous Russian occupation, were fleeing from the area. A new era started with the peaceful entry of the Soviet Army into Czernowitz at the end of March 1944. This was to last two generations, until the dissolution of the Soviet Union and the establishment of Ukraine as an independent country in 1991. There is not a word about the political situation in Martha's letters to Edith. Rather, they are full of stories of survival and tragedy, of 'aunts and uncles' – friends of the family – who had fallen into debt or been taken ill, or worse still, just disappeared.

Martha, and Grandmother Rosa, had endured another desperately hard winter. Martha was still teaching all day every day except Sundays and struggling to adjust to her bereavement. She told Edith that she was so used to seeing Theodor sitting in the large armchair in his woollens next to the stove because he was always cold, that she could hardly believe he was no longer there. It was not until March, when the Russians were entering the city, the snow was melting and the first catkins had appeared, that she made her first visit to his grave.

Many friends and acquaintances were arranging to emigrate whilst they had the opportunity, firstly to Romania and then onward to the United States or Palestine. Martha had given up on the idea of leaving Czernowitz, probably because Rosa, now eighty-six years old, had become too frail to withstand any further upheaval. Thankfully, she was still robust enough to celebrate her birthday in customary style with an almond cake and vanilla *kipferl* – a distraction from bewilderment and fear. As Rosa put it in a letter to Edith, "The whole of life is now a question mark for me."

Edith made every effort to comfort her mother and grandmother, writing frequently to express her hopes about her future life with Ralph in England. In one letter she must even have promised a grandchild, knowing that this was her mother's dearest wish. Martha replied, "Your last letter brought tears to my eyes." She dreamed of seeing Edith in her own home with a baby in her arms – maybe a 'little Theodor'. She hoped that she would be more like a mother than a mother-in-law to Ralph and resolved to improve her English, especially the difficult pronunciation.

Uppermost in Martha's mind was the fate of her sister, Bina and her husband, Emo, Annie's parents. Both she and Edith suspected the terrible truth, that Annie's parents were no longer alive, since stories from the concentration camps were reaching Czernowitz through the grapevine. However, in the absence of any news they could not help hoping for the best. Edith was still sending letters to Bina in the Łódź (Litzmannstadt) ghetto, and Martha asked Edith to find out how she could send money to her. In later life, Annie tried to track the fate of her parents and established that they had died in Auschwitz in the summer of 1943. They must have survived in the ghetto in Łódź for about two years, during which they may well have been forced to work for Rumkowski, the Chairman of the Jewish council within the ghetto, who prolonged the lives of thousands of Jews by providing them with jobs, such as making army uniforms to support the German war effort. This would have kept Annie's parents from starvation or earlier deportation. In May 1944, the entire ghetto was liquidated, and all the surviving inhabitants were sent to the gas chambers in Auschwitz.

*

REINHOLD

Reinhold's time in England proved to be a stroke of tremendous good fortune, representing a turning point in his career. Having practised as a generalist in a remote part of France, where he had become highly skilled and respected, when he found himself in London he was able to seize the opportunity to learn all about anaesthetics, a subject which interested him passionately. In his autobiography, he acknowledges a great debt of gratitude towards the English, even though at the time of writing (1969), Anglophilia was most unfashionable amongst the French because of friction over the Common Market: *plus ça change!*

Reinhold first arrived in Croydon by aeroplane without any papers, fresh from his imprisonment in Spain, to be joined by Fa shortly afterwards. They discovered that all members of the Free French were known to the British authorities and were given a warm welcome. Fa and Reinhold were allowed a few weeks to recover from the hardships they had endured crossing the Pyrenees and Reinhold's internment in Spain. They would always remember the wonderful hospitality and warmth they received from British families, the first in Scotland and the second in Wales, where they spent two idyllic holidays with implausibly perfect weather. Most French soldiers spending any time in Britain during the war came away with very positive feelings towards the British, with one important exception – General de Gaulle himself. Reinhold experienced the British as 'efficient, humane and polite'.

He was rather amused by some British attitudes he noticed: for example, he found out that unmarried couples were not allowed to share a hotel room, yet policemen who were put in charge of shooing away voyeurs and public nuisances in Hyde Park turned a blind eye to the activities of couples behind the bushes. "Ah well," he concluded, "England has always been the country of compromises."

Idleness did not agree with Reinhold. Once back in London, he arranged to work in Westminster Hospital under a thoracic surgeon by the name of Sir Clement Price-Thomas, who was later to operate on King George VI when he had lung cancer. Here, he took the opportunity to observe new techniques in anaesthesia. He was particularly interested in the use of new drugs to alter the patient's level of consciousness. In France at that time, anaesthetics as a speciality did not even exist, and the mainstay was chloroform, often delivered by staff with no training. Reinhold shuddered at the memory of using this to sedate his patients during procedures, since it could so easily have caused sudden death from abnormal heart rhythms.

He threw himself into the study of anaesthetics, burying himself in scientific articles on physiology and pharmacology, and obtained special permission from the Royal College of Physicians to sit the Diploma. Assisting at over one thousand operations, he became the first French doctor to understand the ventilation techniques of modern anaesthetics. In May 1944, just in the nick of time before setting off for Normandy, he managed to sit the diploma examination, but it was not until a good deal later, when back in France, that he found out that he had passed.

During this period, Edith was very fearful for his safety, knowing that he was on the point of returning to France with the Free French forces. She could well imagine that his impetuous temperament would be likely to lead him into danger, or, as she put it, into 'the jaws of Cerberus', the multi-headed hound-monster guarding the gates of Hades. Like Ralph and Bernie, Edith and Reinhold were like chalk and cheese.

Reinhold joined the Juno Beach Sector, leaving England on June 12th 1944, on a ship which formed part of an enormous flotilla of vessels crossing the channel very slowly, protected by Allied forces in the air and under the sea. Two days later, as their native coast came into view, the French let off an uproarious cheer. However, this was premature: the tide was out, and they had to wait for it to come in before disembarking on the beach of Courseulles-sur-Mer. It was then that they suffered terrifying bombardment from the enemy, and although Reinhold's ship did not go under, many soldiers were wounded as they all dived under their vehicles. As they drove onto French soil at Courseulles, he was as tense as a board and his heart was pounding. He then got into an ambulance, and drove straight to the nearest military hospital where, putting his new knowledge into practice, he attended to the wounded.

Reinhold's up-to-date expertise as an anaesthetist was not always appreciated by his French colleagues. Whereas in Bayeux, Normandy, he was regarded as indispensable by the teams working in British-run neurosurgical and maxillofacial units, when he transferred to a French unit in the east of France near the front, the consultant, who knew nothing about modern anaesthesia, was highly suspicious of him. When Reinhold refused to use chloroform, the consultant ordered him to be confined for a week on grounds of insubordination, replacing him in the operating theatre with a nun who had had no training whatsoever.

By the September of 1944, most of France, including Paris, had been liberated. Reinhold visited the capital, commenting wryly that anyone observing the joyful victory celebrations would have thought that the entire population had been members of the Resistance. In his experience, the French army was riddled with anti-Semites. When he was transferred once again to a new unit, he was warned about this by a fellow Jew. True to form, Reinhold confronted his colleagues directly. At the first dinner in the mess, he stood up and announced that he was a foreign Jew who had fought with the Free French, and that he was sure that these facts would not come between him and the rest of them. His words were greeted with a stupefied silence, but he had no problems thereafter.

In the summer of 1944, Reinhold had some leave. On the spur of the moment he decided to visit Annie, his young cousin and protégée, who was in hiding in the Massif Central. The journey proved to be very difficult. He had not bargained for the possibility that simply reaching his destination might take up nearly all his leave. Transport from the north to the south of France was so deficient, partly because of the lack of petrol, that he ended up accepting around forty lifts from assorted vehicles, including milk vans and horse-drawn carts, just to travel the last one hundred kilometres. When he finally arrived in a state of near collapse from exhaustion, Annie, recognising him from a distance in his uniform, came running towards him and flung herself into his arms. On the way back, Reinhold had to make sure he did not run out of leave. This time, he hitched rides on aeroplanes, which took him from Lyon to Brussels and from Brussels back to his regiment in one day. Another example of his boundless chutzpah.

*

ANNIE

Annie was now fifteen years old and had not seen Reinhold or Fa for about eighteen months. The last time she had seen her parents had been when she was nine, when Reinhold had smuggled her into France from a week's skiing holiday in Switzerland. Little did she know when her parents, Bina and Emo, put her on the train at the Austro-Swiss border with Reinhold in January 1939, that she would never see them again.

When they left France to escape to Spain, Reinhold and Fa had entrusted Annie into the care of their colleague, Dr Daniel Eyraud. This arrangement saved Annie's life for the third time. The Eyrauds were pious Protestants, who had been established in the Massif Central for a long time. The region served as a good hiding place for dissidents of all sorts because of its inaccessibility, particularly during the winter snows. Generations of Protestants continued with their austere existence in an enclosed community, keeping up their traditions, and a spirit of dissent. As a persecuted group within the state, their sympathies during the Second World War leant naturally towards the Jews. It was therefore perhaps not surprising that the whole area was a hotbed of the Resistance and a centre for the sheltering and assistance of hundreds of Jewish children.

In September 1943, Annie went to live with a cousin of Dr Eyraud in a home for Jewish children called *Les Ombrages* in the village of Le Chambon-sur-Lignon. Dr Eyraud had arranged for her to have a false name and identity papers from a town in which the archive had been destroyed by fire. In Le Chambon-sur-Lignon, she continued her education along with hundreds of other Jewish children at the secondary school, the École Nouvelle Cévenol, founded by the two pastors of the village, Monsieur Trocmé and Monsieur Theis, in 1938.

In her autobiography, *Quitter Vienne*, Annie describes her emotions during this phase of her life, when she was thrown into a group of adolescent boys and girls, none of whom knew what had happened to their parents. She remembers it as an idyllic time, when they all repressed their fears and lived in the present. She quotes from a Hungarian writer, Imre Kertész,[13] that 'it is not easy to extinguish the joie de vivre of a fourteen-year-old child.' Happiness for her at that time consisted in tobogganing in a procession of sledges at dangerous speed down the snowy slopes to school in the morning, skiing at weekends with a group of friends, going on delightful long treks and picnics in the mountains during the summer and her first experience of passionate adolescent love.

Annie was dimly aware of the active part played by the whole community in the Resistance, and of strange goings on at night in the house, when she was awoken by what sounded like people tramping up and down the stairs. She felt safer if she did not ask any questions. Once, she recalled, she was woken in the middle of the night, to be taken on a long walk deep into the woods. Suddenly, there was a deafening roar and she was practically knocked over by a strong gust of wind. As she looked up, there, right above her, was a parachutist jumping out of an aeroplane. Horrified, she saw the man landing, followed by boxes of weapons falling from the aeroplane. She remembered having to help gather up the voluminous swathes of material from the parachute, which later were used to make shirts.

Another uncomfortable factor during Annie's life at Le Chambon-sur-Lignon was the presence of German soldiers in the town. In fact, there was a bevy of them convalescing from the Eastern Front in the hotel right in the middle of the village, literally next door to another home full of Jewish children and just across the street from *Les Ombrages* where Annie was staying. Encountering these soldiers walking down the streets in their Wehrmacht uniforms was disconcerting to say the least, but they were really quite friendly. Did they realise how many Jewish children were being sheltered right under their noses? Perhaps they were so traumatised by their experiences in Russia that they chose to turn a blind eye to the situation. Annie told me that she had heard that a group of village lads had been planning to kill the German soldiers whilst they were bathing in the river. Luckily their plot had reached the ears of members of the Resistance, who had prevented it, thereby averting complete disaster. Undoubtedly the resulting exposure would have led to the wholesale massacre of all the hidden Jewish children in the Massif, and the execution of the Resistance members and their families. Just a few months afterwards, the retreating German army murdered 642 men women and children from the village of Oradour-sur-Glane in the most sadistic manner.

In retrospect, Annie came to realise how near to danger she had been living in Le Chambon-sur-Lignon. Daniel Trocmé, a cousin of the Pastor, had been arrested, along with eighteen students, in the summer of 1943, before Annie's arrival. By the time she came to live there, the subversive activities of the villagers would already have been known to the German authorities. It was only long after the war that she learned that her host, Leon Eyraud, had been the head of the local Resistance and that, all the while, he had been storing cases of guns and ammunition in the cellar of *Les Ombrages*. Annie passed the first part of the Baccalaureate just as the war was ending and was soon able to rejoin her cousins Reinhold and Fa, who became her adoptive parents.

*

BERNIE

Ralph was much more confident about his brother, Bernie, than Edith was about Reinhold. Bernie would come home safely: he was tough and had learned how to defend himself as a member of a street gang when he was growing up in the East End of London. Bernie was keeping the family informed and entertained about the war with a flow of postcards marked 'FROM ACTIVE SERVICE' as he progressed from Normandy to Belgium. In fact, both he and Reinhold were in Bayeux at around the same time, had they but known it.

Bernie wrote that he had spent one week in Cherbourg before moving on to Bayeux. "Travelling at speed army style isn't exactly first class. I spent most of the first day trying to balance a box of rations on my head, at the same time giving nasty looks and a bit of my tongue to a laddie who was breathing heavily down my left ear." He was not far from Caen at the time of the

Germans' defeat and passed through the *bocage* or 'hedgerows' country in Normandy, where there was heavy fighting. Bernie made no mention to his family of the shrapnel wound in his foot which was to trouble him for the rest of his life.

The destination of Bernie's battalion was Flanders. According to him, they were the first troops to arrive there after the 'P.B.I.' ('poor bloody infantry'). This indicates that he was in a pioneer battalion, whose remit was to restore damaged bridges and roads. They stopped in a 'loverly (*sic*) Flemish town' where they were given a tumultuous welcome. Bernie had revelled in the journey. "Every day I tried a new position in the vans until I finished up near the tailboard, the best position of the lot. Although this meant someone standing on my feet all the time, I was able to see where I had come from and wave to cheering crowds."

Life had been very hard in Flanders during the German occupation. According to Bernie, rationing had been so severe, and food so scarce, that the people had resorted to eating rats. On arrival at the lovely town in Flanders, Bernie and his mates were mobbed by some overjoyed locals, who took them through their house into their garden, where there was an enormous peach tree laden with ripe fruit. "I didn't believe it. I picked one to see if it was real. Immediately our hosts began filling our pockets, while an old lady gave us a cat's lick with a flannel. Next, we found ourselves drinking glass after glass of cognac, shaking hands, giving autographs, dancing, singing and going mad in general! The people seemed to be stark raving mad with joy. We stopped to make enquiries, and in a jiffy, we were yanked off our lorry and bundled into homes all the way down the street."

Bernie's time in Flanders continued in this vein. The locals did not charge the soldiers for travel – after all, if the Germans would not pay, why should they? Beer was a mere four pence per glass and soldiers were given the best seats in the cinema.

Flemish people were so very friendly and always eager to try out their English. "Everyone seems to have swotted up on English in a hurry. It's nothing to be greeted with 'Good night' at eight o'clock in the morning and children rushed up and said 'Goodbye' when they meant 'Hello'". At any rate, communication was never a problem for Bernie: he explained that "Flemish is ten percent like Yiddish and ten percent like bad English, so in a fashion, we understand each other".

11

TYING THE KNOT

1945 proved to be very eventful for Edith. After several months of intense preparation at the Berne Conservatoire, she sat the Concert Diploma examination in February. The whole experience was gruelling, and the strain took its toll. Shortly beforehand, she wrote to Ralph, "My nerves are ruined, and life seems too difficult. I feel at the end of my tether. Anyway, I will let you know everything. Even if I fail you will still accept me, won't you?"

The examination itself was extremely arduous: in the morning Edith performed two solo concerts, followed by a piece of chamber music, the *Trout Quintet* by Schubert. That same evening, she gave a public recital on the piano in the main hall of the Conservatoire. The extensive programme, which she performed by heart, consisted of nine pieces including works by Bach, Beethoven, Brahms, Chopin, Debussy and Ravel. Afterwards, when, not surprisingly, she was in a state of near collapse, a feeling of despondency came over her, because she felt that she had not played her best, and she knew that if she failed, she would not be allowed a second attempt. The panel of external judges, three of the most eminent musicians in Switzerland, passed her unanimously.

After her success in the Concert Diploma, Edith enrolled in a musicology class at the university and resumed her studies with Franz Josef Hirt, joining his class for professional concert artists, where they explored the complete piano sonatas of Beethoven and the Debussy *Preludes*. However, Edith was now finding it difficult to concentrate on the piano. At this point, all she really wanted was to be reunited with Ralph. She lost no time in applying for a French visa with the intention of leaving Switzerland as soon as possible, exclaiming to Ralph, "If you could come to Paris, even for twenty-four hours on leave, I would do the impossible to get to Paris as soon as possible if I was certain of finding you there. We will talk and talk and catch up on the long years so rich in events and experiences."

Whilst waiting for her visa, Edith was engaged to play in four concerts, one of which was a lecture-recital. As she was still not allowed to earn any money because of her status as a refugee, they were all free or given in aid of charity. There seemed to be no shortage of openings for Edith's career. She had opportunities to perform Chopin and Beethoven piano concertos in September, by which time she fervently hoped to have left the country. A short holiday in Davos, staying with an old friend of her mother's, helped Edith to relax and recover from her ordeal. She told Ralph that she always took one of his letters with her wherever she went as a 'talisman', adding ecstatically, "If only you could see the mountains crowned with snow against the deep blue sky..." Whilst in Davos, she started to experiment in the kitchen with culinary delights she was planning to make for Ralph. One of their favourites was *crème de marrons* (chestnut purée) with whipped cream.

Ralph was delighted to hear that Edith had passed the Concert Diploma. Congratulating her on her brilliant success, he shared the good news that he was to be promoted again, this time to the rank of major, and was expecting to be posted to

France or Germany very soon. He put in a request to be sent to France, hoping this would make it easier to meet Edith. There is a tantalising hole cut out of this letter by the censor, where for once, Ralph might have overstepped the mark by discussing his war work. Knowing Ralph was back in London made Edith very fearful for his safety. News had reached her of the flying bombs, and she had just read that the Allies had found a gigantic mine full of V2 rockets in Germany camouflaged in a forest, destined for the destruction of London.

Ralph made a point of attending a concert given by Edith's former teacher, Yvonne Lefébure, who was on tour. Knowing that Edith would be eager for every detail, he wrote her a 'blow by blow' account of Miss Lefébure's performance at the Royal Albert Hall in front of a packed audience of five thousand people. Ralph thought she looked very glamourous in a full-length, dark brown velvet concert dress with turquoise passementerie at the sleeves, set off by a chunky turquoise necklace and complemented by her golden hair plaited in coils around her head. She found the piano stool too low, which sent a member of staff scurrying off to find a solution. He returned with a thick pile of music for Miss Lefébure to sit on. Her interpretation of Beethoven's fourth piano concerto with the London Philharmonic Orchestra was 'astonishing'.

Afterwards, Ralph went into the Green Room, where, from close up, Yvonne seemed drawn and haggard under her make-up, expending a lot of nervous energy talking to her admirers about those of her musical colleagues in France who were collaborators. Alfred Cortot was a notable example. Yvonne herself had refused to be considered a member of the Paris Conservatoire under the Germans. When Ralph eventually managed to speak to Yvonne on her own, she was fulsome in her affection and regard for Edith. Shortly after this concert in the Albert Hall, Yvonne also performed a programme of French music, old and new, at the Wigmore Hall, under the patronage of the French Ambassador.

Judging from their correspondence, it seems that it was becoming an increasing struggle for Ralph and Edith to maintain meaningful communication during this time. This could not be attributed simply to the vagaries of the postal system. Edith noted sadly that Ralph's letters were getting shorter and seemed lacking in warmth. She herself found it difficult to express herself fully on paper. "There is so much we cannot discuss in letters – so much which preoccupies and torments us. I realise my letters are not what you want them to be."

He, in turn, felt he was getting out of touch, repeatedly asking her for more information about her daily life. She replied with a detailed letter, revealing how unsociable and self-sufficient she had become. A typical day for Edith went like this: she usually got up at 7am, settling down at the piano after housework and breakfast at around nine. She worked until twelve (with cigarette breaks) and then listened to the news and read the papers over lunch. After black coffee and a cigarette, she was back at the piano until tea, then she would check the post to see if there was a letter from Ralph, returning to the piano until six-thirty. In the evening she made herself a little supper, and after any washing and ironing, ensconced herself in her red armchair, listening to the radio or with a book and a pack of cigarettes. Currently she was absorbed in a biography of St Exupéry, who had recently died in a flying mission for the Resistance over occupied France in July 1944. Regrettably, Edith had taken up smoking whilst she was working with such intensity for the diploma. She was hoping to succeed in giving up the vice when she finally reached Paris, since she had heard that women did not have cigarette rations there. She realised how lonely she was feeling. "Life without the presence of a single person who is dear to one, life without affection amongst strangers, however well-meaning is hard." Although she had many acquaintances, there were only a few people she could really talk to and for her, there were only really four people who counted: Ralph, Reinhold, her mother and Yvonne.

Ralph frequently tried to encourage Edith to socialise more and to make more friends. Her response was that she had given up on this. She had very little in common with most Swiss women. "Just imagine," she exclaimed, "that when the possibility of giving them the vote was discussed, they were not in favour because they regarded the sole aim of their life as homemaking." Everything in the life of a Swiss woman was focused on marriage. So, the alternative was to have friendships with men, but this was tricky. "If they are serious, friendships turn into love and that is quite natural and, alas, I know how dangerous that is." Hinting at problems she had faced, she continued, "This last year has brought me the most illusions and disillusion which I haven't quite recovered from."

This comment pushed Ralph into asking a direct question. Had Edith been unfaithful to him? Although she replied that she would be completely frank, what she wrote is ambiguous and difficult to interpret. Clearly nothing took place between her and Herr Hirt on a physical level. Edith assured Ralph that she had not been unfaithful and that she would not be capable of writing to him if she had been. Yet she admits, "I was tormented, I really suffered. With your sensitivity, you guessed this without my having to tell you. I must ask you to allow me to tell you everything when we meet but my attachment for you remains whole and intact. Is that not enough, isn't that all that counts? I have great need for your affection." She hoped that she had set his mind at rest and that all the problems caused by their separation would be resolved when they met again.

My feeling is that Herr Hirt had fallen in love with Edith, which would have created an extremely stressful situation for her, since he had the power to influence her career. This seems quite likely, judging from the extravagant praise and encouragement he gave her. Whereas Yvonne, for example, had told her that her playing was not mature enough to tackle the Beethoven fourth piano concerto, Herr Hirt had told her that it was 'as if Beethoven had written it for her!' Maybe such flattery had been hard to resist. Edith might have had some reason to feel guilty, if it had been only in thought, that she had betrayed Ralph. The disillusion she referred to might have come about if Herr Hirt made life unpleasant for her when rejected. All this is conjecture: however, it illustrates, not for the first time, that where the writer of a letter is not telling the whole story, this is generally sensed by the recipient.

Ralph must have reassured her in a subsequent letter. She felt immense gratitude towards him and relief that he was prepared to love her as she was. It was pointless to hide her weaknesses from him. She was missing her mother, from whom she had heard nothing for nearly a year since the Soviet reoccupation of Czernowitz. At times she felt so 'small and weak' that she craved her mother's blind love and Ralph's protection. She was able to express this because she understood he reciprocated the same great need for unconditional acceptance. She asked him to 'extend his hand' so that she could cross the abyss towards him with an 'internal visa'.

However, the months were passing, and by April, Edith had still not received her French visa. Agitated and impatient, knowing that Ralph might be sent abroad at any time, and that there was a danger of missing the opportunity to see him, she set off for the French Consulate in Geneva to request a week's transit pass to Paris, since only French citizens were permitted to return to France permanently. Her application was turned down. Edith then decided to take the law into her own hands. This backfired and she was arrested on the twenty-fifth of April when attempting to cross the border illegally in the region of Bardonnex in the Canton of Geneva, where she was interned again for a week in a camp at a place called Claparède. Poor Edith had risked her life getting into Switzerland and was now unable to leave. Swallowing her disappointment, she made light of the episode to Ralph. "You will have heard of my misadventures from my brother. Let's not talk any more about it. It all turned out well, because I was permitted to return to Berne to continue my studies at the Conservatoire. Forever, Edith."

Undeterred by this unfortunate experience, Edith persisted in pursuing her plan to go to Paris. Reinhold was now there, so she was able to enlist his help in completing the formalities. At last she received permission to travel. Ralph had warned her about the difficulties of life in Paris. Everything cost 'an arm and a leg' even though food was of very poor quality. In December there had been an alarming number of deaths caused by lack of food and heating. Edith replied that "it would still be their dear Paris, even if their *Cité Universitaire* was no longer given over to students." Ralph had informed her that he was to be posted to Germany in the coming few months. Edith was glad that he would be of use in the Allied Occupation and asked him whether she might be able to join him there. She was trying to suppress feelings of hatred, having some sympathy for the German people, as one who, herself, had been forced to submit to the Nazi regime. She realised that it might nevertheless be quite a sacrifice for Ralph to have to put his academic career on hold until he was no longer required in Germany.

Ralph duly received the all-important telegram delivered to the flat in Hackney: "Will be in Paris on 19th May 1945." The six years of separation were about to end. It is hard to imagine the degree of tension and the tangle of emotions they must have experienced before this long-awaited moment. For each of them, the image of the other had sustained them through periods of loneliness, fear and hopelessness. There were times when they had doggedly clung to their relationship even when it must have seemed like a fantasy. While it is probably fair to say that more conventional people might have gone their separate ways after such a long period of time, they had both had strong motivation for their commitment. Ralph, as a homosexual, felt no interest in other women sexually, whilst Edith, being such a loner, was able to survive by creating and holding onto an inner, idealised vision of the man she had loved.

They must have spent a few days in Paris together, when they were able to discuss the future, and the realities of marriage in England in a way they had not been able to do before. It was also an opportunity to unburden themselves of all the issues they had felt unable to put down on paper. Ralph probably told Edith about his war work which he had guarded so carefully from the censors. She could have explained what had been so complicated and painful about her relationship with her teacher, Franz Josef Hirt. Most importantly, I think that Ralph would have kept his promise and found it a great relief to tell Edith the whole truth about his sexuality, which in letters he had always alluded to as his 'psychological problem'.

How I wish I could relate that this meeting was full of simple joy. Sadly, this was not the case. It was clearly complicated for them both. On his return to London, Ralph wrote to Edith, as if continuing their discussion: "I am still of the opinion that the best thing for us is to get married. If you insist on waiting for a great love to develop that may never happen, you will be sacrificing the substance for the shadow." There was not much time to make this decision because he was expecting to be sent to Germany at short notice.

I know, from repeated conversations with Ralph years later, that he was disappointed with Edith at this momentous meeting. With characteristic tactlessness, he had no qualms about telling his daughter about the lack of chemistry between them. He was taken aback when he saw that Edith had put on weight (on her Swiss identity card she was described as 'of solid build') and that her lonely and austere lifestyle, 'on a diet', as he put it 'of frankfurters and sauerkraut', had changed her. Now aged thirty-one, after all her ordeals, she was no longer the lively young woman in her early twenties he remembered. Nevertheless, he had made the decision that he must 'be normal' and was given to rationalising his union with Edith by repeating, 'If I couldn't be happy myself, at least I could make someone else happy.'

Edith immediately applied for a British visa, which she received remarkably quickly, in addition to a new Romanian passport. Before leaving Paris, she managed to meet her beloved teacher, Yvonne Lefébure, and then made a quick visit to Bussières, the first since her escape to Switzerland in 1942, to collect some important documents and a suitcase of books. At the end of June, Ralph received a further telegram informing him that Edith was landing at Newhaven on 1st July 1945 and would be arriving at Victoria Station in London at 9.30pm.

Ralph and Edith's wedding took place in haste at Hackney Town Hall on 6th July 1945, just five days after Edith's arrival in England. There are a few wedding photographs. One shows three of Ralph's female cousins, two of them linking arms with Edith, who looks pretty and happy, wearing a fashionable hat. The velvet dress borrowed from one of the cousins is a reasonable, but not a perfect, fit. A second photograph shows Ralph and Edith together with two of the cousins. It is not possible to gauge Ralph's emotions in this one, since the photographer, one of the cousins, managed to decapitate him. All of Edith is visible since, being so much shorter than Ralph, she only reached up to his shoulder.

Edith was soon introduced to Ralph's large extended family, developing a good rapport with his warm-hearted cousins,

Rose and Sandra. Then, after only ten days of marriage, Ralph left for Germany to serve with the British Army of the Rhine. Edith and Ralph were back again to what they knew best: separation. However, Ralph's letters to Edith from Germany show new warmth and intimacy. His first letter, on arrival at the headquarters of the Control Commission for Germany, addressed to 'My dear wife' is full of the wonder he felt at seeing the clouds during his first experience of travelling by air. Further letters are very matrimonial in content: he thanked her for the sheets, razor blades and a delicious cake which he shared with fellow officers in the mess. Could she send him a dressing gown? Soon after he arrived in Germany, he wanted to know if she had missed her period. "You say nothing about your biological processes, so I assume all is back to normal – too bad!" This was sheer impatience on his part, as it would have still been too early for Edith to know whether she was pregnant, but it indicates this was planned, at least by him. A few weeks later, Edith complained to her doctor-brother that she was feeling sick all the time. The revelation that she was pregnant was a terrible shock to her. She must have conceived within a few days of the wedding, as the baby was due in early April 1946.

Ralph was sometimes taken aback by Edith's absent-mindedness in everyday life. On one occasion he thanked her for sending him his pyjama top, but could she please look for the bottom which must be in the flat somewhere as he was not in the habit of travelling with only one half of a pair. Edith was discovering that he was apt to lose his temper, after which he was always penitent. "I regret infinitely, my dearest, that I caused you pain. Try to forget anything disagreeable that happened during my leave – just think that the 'Schlechter Bube' (bad boy) could have been much more 'schlecht'."

Although, for some reason, Ralph did not preserve any of Edith's letters to him during this period, it is not difficult to surmise from his comments that she was struggling to adapt to her new life. Having waited for Ralph for six years, she found herself on her own again, after only ten days of marriage. The prospect of not having him home again, apart from short periods of leave, for possibly another year was hard enough, but she also had to adjust to a new country and language for the fourth time in her short life. Furthermore, she found herself keeping house for an elderly man in a run-down, ramshackle flat in Hackney, for, despite his intentions, Ralph had not been able to find any other accommodation. From time to time, Bernie, Ralph's bachelor brother, appeared when he was on leave. The scenario is rather reminiscent of Harold Pinter's play, *The Homecoming*. To cap it all, Edith was afflicted with the dreadful nausea and malaise of early pregnancy. Ralph exhorted her not to spend too much time in the kitchen and hoped that his father was not making her go short of housekeeping money. She would, by now, have received her identity card and her ration cards for food and clothes.

It goes without saying that Ralph was utterly delighted, when in September 1945, he learned that he was going to be a father. However, the miserable letters from Edith, in which she told him how ill she was feeling, filled him with dismay. His advice was to drink a lot of water and milk, take plenty of sugar and most importantly, to keep her bowels open. Before he had left, Ralph had made sure to install a piano in the flat for Edith. Now she was feeling so low that she had lost all inspiration and motivation to play, and Ralph's attempts to reassure her that this would soon pass were all in vain. Her suggestion that she come out to join him in Germany was, he said, 'out of the question'. He must have discussed Edith's plight with the family network of kindly female relatives. Aunt Sylvia helpfully came up with the solution of employing a cleaning lady.

Ralph was most concerned that Edith should take steps to develop her career as a concert pianist. Although he envisaged that she would also have to supplement their income with some private teaching, he was confident of her potential as a performing artist. She had already made some important contacts, including 'the ear', as Ralph put it, of Edward Lockspeiser, the English musicologist and expert on Debussy. She had also met and played to the renowned pianist, Louis Kentner, who was favourably impressed.

Ralph, now Major Leigh, was settling down in the Secretariat of the Chief of Staff of the British Zone in the Control Commission for Germany. His work took him to Berlin and to the industrial Ruhr region, but mostly to the small town of Lübbecke in the north of the country about seventy-five kilometres west of Hanover. In September he attended the Lüneberg trials for a day, hearing evidence from 'the brutes of Belsen', where fifteen of the forty-five defendants were acquitted.

Even more distressing to Ralph than the wholesale physical ruin of the city of Berlin, was the evident destruction of the morale of its inhabitants. One of his assignments was to survey the extent of the devastation of the Ruhr area with a group of colleagues. They found it impossible to visit several of the places on their itinerary because of broken bridges, reporting that while Düsseldorf, Dortmund and Essen were badly smashed, Cologne had received the worst damage of all. He commented that: "People did not look underfed although pale – one explanation is that they lived very much in cellars and in the recent wet weather only came out when necessary to get food."

On his return to Lübbecke, Ralph was very busy, apparently enjoying the work, although he did not reveal what he was doing. In his archive, I found a document addressed to the Chief of Staff, presumably Ralph's superior, handwritten and signed by B. L. Montgomery, Field Marshal British Zone, in which he asked for a report on the activity of members of the German clergy, for submission to the Archbishop of Canterbury, with a view to involving them in the future reconstruction of Germany.

Ralph wrote an official report of his impressions of Lübbecke, in which he makes comparisons between small-town life in England and Germany, highlighting some local peculiarities. "Chimney sweeps wear top hats, a startling sight on their bicycles, complete with brushes and shining topper." Children (who seemed to form three-quarters of the population of Germany) were all "flaxen-haired, blue-eyed little Aryans" who "invariably greet us with enquiring cries of *Shokolat? Zigarette?*"

Ralph told the following story, which he felt was most revealing about the attitude of Germans. It took place in the Officers' Club. "A German waiter was inveighing against the wicked Nazis who brought ruin upon the innocent Germans.

"British Officer: 'But in the old days you too shouted "Heil Hitler", didn't you?'

"Indignant waiter: 'Of course, while everything was going well!'"

Whilst serving in Germany, Ralph was also planning his future career in Britain. He had continued to work for his cousin's publishing business, submitting freelance stories for *The Dandy McQueen* children's comic to bring in extra money, whilst completing his thesis on Jean-Jacques Rousseau. He had decided that school teaching was not for him, and that he would apply for academic posts. Although he had responded to an advertisement for employment in the Civil Service, he confessed to Edith that he was sure that he would not even be considered, however well qualified he might be, because of his Russian-born Jewish father. The Civil Service had relaxed its rules of employment in 1930, stipulating that parents of applicants need not have been born in Britain, but were required to have naturalised as British citizens. This was probably not the case with Ralph's father.

Towards the end of 1945, Edith was beginning to feel more settled in her new country. She had entered the second trimester of her pregnancy, and Ralph had been home on leave. No doubt her English was becoming more fluent and she was getting to know the family better. She had also managed a successful recital in Bath. But most important of all, she was now able to visit her mother, who had reached Paris and was staying with Reinhold and Fa. Just how Martha had made her way from Soviet-ruled Czernowitz to the West is another story.

12

THE CZERNOWITZ
ADVENTURE

The war was over for Edith and Ralph, now Mr and Mrs Leigh, and for Reinhold and Fa. But their joy was mixed with the anxiety that they might never see Martha again, since it was not officially possible to travel into or out of the Soviet Union. Martha was now living alone in Czernowitz. Theodor had died in 1943, and Rosa, her mother, must have died sometime after the Soviet reoccupation. Since there had not been any communication between Martha and her children for over a year, there is no mention in the family archive as to when and how Rosa had died.

In the summer of 1945, Reinhold was still serving in the French army. He was sent to Vienna ahead of his colleagues from their base in a sanatorium in the Black Forest. His boss, the Chief Medical Officer, asked him to prepare for the unit to establish itself as the surgical service in the French sector of the occupying forces. "You won't be there on your own for long," he said reassuringly. "We will join you after a few days." He chose Reinhold for this mission because of his knowledge of German. Reinhold's stay in Vienna provided him with an opportunity to rescue his mother from Czernowitz. This chapter is a translation from his autobiography *Mes quatre vies*, in which he describes this great adventure. His writing style displays his supreme self-confidence and the story, his exceptional fearlessness.

*

Vienna was in the middle of Russian-occupied territory. Communications were limited, or to put it more accurately, non-existent. Entrusted formally with this mission, accompanied by another doctor and a nurse, I set off into the unknown. First, we travelled by train, and then we were picked up by car. My mission document cut no ice at all with representatives of the Allied powers' military police. I had to use the utmost persuasiveness at several frontiers, and after three days arrived in Vienna. In contrast to the villages we had passed through in the Black Forest, which had practically escaped the ravages of war, and where the French occupation was tolerated quite easily, we found Vienna to have been mercilessly crushed into a state of submission by the Russians. They were not going to forget the ferocious acts of the Germans on their territory and behaved like conquerors: Russian men considered themselves above the law, taking women as the victors' prize. Anything could be removed, requisitioned or destroyed at any moment.

An early summer heatwave pounded down on the city. The streets were practically deserted. You could read fear in the faces of the few people you encountered. The last mass conscription had mobilised all men capable of holding a gun, including adolescents. We only came across old men and children. The women were terrified, emerging from indoors just to buy food, which itself was very difficult to obtain. Three months of occupation had brought famine to Vienna.

I was now in an unusual situation, as one of the first Western officers to have entered Vienna under the Russian Occupation. The Austrians received me as if I was a liberator, in which they were mistaken. The Russian authorities, with whom I was to have a lot of dealings, also welcomed me most cordially. At that time, relationships between the Allies were still harmonious. We were a long way from the Cold War.

One of my first visits was to meet the Russian general, the governor of the city. Despite my lowly rank of lieutenant, he regarded me as representing France and treated me accordingly. He immediately summoned the mayor and the Austrian prefect, announcing in a highly intimidating fashion, "From now on, any order given by Lieutenant Kern should be considered as coming from me."

From that day, I experienced the power of that simple piece of equipment, the telephone, when the person at the other end of the line is seized with terror. With one simple call, everything, and I mean absolutely anything, was at my disposal, even things which were supposedly impossible to find in this city of Vienna, which had been emptied out by five years of war and three months of pillaging.

I requisitioned a private clinic containing everything necessary to perform surgery, even a state-of-the-art X-ray machine. All of this had apparently escaped Russian scrutiny. When he was informed about my activities, the Russian Chief Medical Officer arrived the following day to inspect this modern hospital. On realising what a discovery I had made, he pulled a long face which revealed his disappointment at not having found it himself. Still, despite the apprehensiveness of the Austrians, he left everything intact, and all the instruments were still in place on the day my unit eventually arrived in Vienna to start work.

This day was far longer in coming than I had been led to believe by my boss. My unit had been transferred to the Tyrol, where the officers had taken a liking to hunting for chamois. They were quite aware of conditions in Vienna and were in no hurry to join me there. I stayed there on my own for six long weeks, cut off from everything, receiving no post or instructions, money or food. As the only French doctor, I had to cope with multiple problems. I found myself representing my country in anything that had to do with medicine or public health, including combatting venereal disease and typhus.

Some officers from other Allied countries arrived. When I discussed matters with them, I went to bed at English bedtime, but I had to get up at the time it was in Moscow to deal with the Russians. This meant that I had a twenty-hour day. Once I had completed my organisational duties, I had to tackle my administrative work. I took notes and started files, because being a soldier, I had to document all my actions.

I established excellent relations with the French Mission, composed of a few high-ranking officers under the command of the General Ch***, who understood the enormous scope of the work I was undertaking and was most appreciative. This stood me in good stead, which I can vouch for later in this story.

The sixth week had just gone by. At last my unit arrived. The hospital was ready to open its doors. I had also managed to secure sumptuous rooms, or requisition villas for my colleagues. I allowed myself to comment to my boss, the Chief Medical Officer, that he had rather abandoned me. He replied, smiling, "Oh I knew that you wouldn't really need us here and that you would manage fine on your own!"

The post had arrived with the unit. There were several letters from my wife. Enclosed in one of them was a message in my mother's hand, which she had entrusted in Czernowitz to a Belgian prisoner who was being repatriated via Odessa. This message, which had taken two months to reach me, informed me that my mother had finally succeeded in obtaining authorisation to leave Russian-occupied Czernowitz to join her sister in Timişoara, Romania. After the premature death of my father during the war, my mother had stayed in Czernowitz to look after my aged grandmother. Once she had died, there was nothing to keep my mother in the town of her birth any longer.

Timişoara is six or seven hundred kilometres from Vienna. To reach it, you would have to cross two countries, Czechoslovakia and Hungary. An idea occurred to me which soon became a decision: I must go and collect my mother from Timişoara. I knew that a short time previously, a small branch of the French Red Cross had been established in Budapest. I arranged for a Red Cross ambulance, along with two charming female drivers, to be allocated to me, so that I could carry out an assignment in Budapest. I added Timişoara, Romania, to the itinerary. Petrol in Vienna was like gold dust. But General Ch***, whom I have already mentioned, arranged for me to have a petrol coupon. I set off on this expedition with confidence. It seemed straightforward. Sure enough, everything went according to plan and I crossed all the borders without any problems, arriving in Timişoara after two days.

My aunt, who was not expecting me, and with whom I had lost all contact for many years, did not recognise me as her nephew when I appeared out of the blue at her door. But blood is thicker than water. Once she had recovered from the initial shock, she received me with heartfelt joy. Unfortunately, I was in for a bitter disappointment. All authorisations to leave the Soviet Union had been cancelled. My mother was stuck in Czernowitz and did not know if she would ever be able to leave.

I discovered that in Timişoara there was a French Consulate which, since Romania had never been at war with France, had remained open. When I presented myself there, the consul was quite taken aback to find himself face to face with a French officer. I informed him that I had an ambulance at my disposal and asked him how I could make myself useful. "Since you mention it," he replied, "at the gates of the city there is a camp of German prisoners of war. We have noticed that there are several people from Alsace who were forced into the German army, some of whom are seriously ill."

I spent that evening with my family, and the two ambulance women. Having been cut off from all communication with the West, my relations bombarded me with questions. It was very late by the time I got to bed. Early the next morning, I introduced myself to the Russian officer in command of the prisoner-of-war camp. Showing him my written commission, I told him that I had been charged with repatriating the sickest people from Alsace. He must have been convinced that I was telling the truth because of the ambulance and the two ambulance women. We took six Alsatians out of the infirmary, and immediately set off back on the same route and deposited them in a hospital in Vienna.

As we approached Vienna, a new idea was forming in my mind. My trip to Romania had proved easy; we were in the aftermath of war and Central Europe was calm. It occurred to me that I could take advantage of this situation. The biggest hurdle, once I had crossed the countries of Central Europe, would be crossing the border with Russia, where the dreaded N.K.V.D. – the secret police – operated. Unauthorised entry into Russia was an extremely serious offence, and highly risky for anyone attempting it. Invariably, one would be suspected of spying. The culprit would most likely to be sent to Siberia or would simply 'disappear'. Weighing up the pros and cons of this situation was difficult. On the one hand I would have to undergo great danger, on the other, my mother would have to remain in captivity, possibly at the expense of her life.

I was devoted to my mother and fervently wanted to find her alive. I had dreamed of making sure that the last years of her life were happy. The hand of fate that had taken me to Vienna seemed to open an opportunity. Furthermore, I had already succeeded in several ventures which, when considered rationally, might have seemed like utter madness, so that little by little, I had convinced myself that I would be successful in anything I attempted. However, this did not mean that I was oblivious to the obstacles which would arise on an expedition to Russia. The first challenge was how to travel such a long distance and how to obtain enough fuel for the journey.

I requested and was granted a meeting with the General Ch***. I put my cards on the table and explained the project to him. I implored him to give me special permission to do it, asking for his help. The General was a generous man who behaved with integrity, never shirking his obligations. He quickly grasped the situation, but then he took a little while to think about it. He replied, "I have seen how much good work you have done here. You have also brought six sick Alsatian men back to Vienna. All this deserves recompense. I am therefore disposed to cover you on behalf of the French Authorities. I am also happy to give you my help to enable you to execute your plan. But you will be taking huge risks, and you must understand that if you are arrested by the Russians, I will be obliged to declare that I knew nothing about the whole affair."

As soon as I left the General, I started my preparations. There was no question of taking the Red Cross ambulance driven by the two women. On the other hand, it would be extremely foolhardy to set off on a journey of hundreds of kilometres on my own, with my rudimentary knowledge of mechanics. I summoned Roger C., my faithful driver. "I have been charged with a special mission, not without danger. I know that you have been demobilised and that you are due to return to France soon. I would like you to accompany me, but I can't make you do this, you have to decide of your own free will." Without any hesitation, he replied, "Wherever you go, Lieutenant, I will go with you!" "Thank you so much. You have always been so loyal I didn't expect anything else from you. But this will be a long expedition, and the vehicle needs to be in perfect condition. I'd like to give you a week to give it a complete overhaul and to renew any old parts as necessary. Also, I need your absolute discretion about this. No-one must know what we are planning."

I had a document typed up, commissioning me to go to as far as Budapest, to which I added Czernowitz, after having tracked down, with some difficulty, a typewriter with a Cyrillic keyboard. I added as many stamps as I could lay my hands on, even though they had nothing whatsoever to do with that kind of assignment. They looked very impressive, especially the one with the hammer and sickle in the middle of a five-pointed star.

It was crucial for me to decide on the best route. Obviously, any official worth his salt would immediately be able to detect that my document was fraudulent. To avoid such people, I would have to take small roads – roads in a poor state of repair, across territory where there had been serious fighting. These sorts of places would probably be controlled by ordinary occupying troops. Accordingly, I devised an itinerary which would take me across Hungary, sub-Carpathian Russia and Galicia, to reach northern Bukovina.

The appointed day arrived. I made my driver empty his pockets, only permitting him to keep on his person his Viennese identity card as a member of the French occupying troops. Not a single piece of paper, not even the most precious of letters from his fiancée, should accompany him on this journey, so that no incriminating document could be taken from him if we were arrested. I brought reserves of tinned food to take with us. I was thinking that this would not only keep us going but might also be useful as currency. Roger assured me that the vehicle was in perfect working order and he had also stocked up with several spare tyres. In addition, I had filled as many containers with petrol as we could accommodate, again with the afterthought that this could come in useful for bartering.

We set off. All my driver knew was that we were heading for Bratislava and then onwards to Budapest. He forbore from asking me a single indiscreet question. By the third day, however, when it had become obvious that we were heading east, he began to guess our destination. We passed through the Czech, Slovakian and Hungarian borders without having to undergo any rigorous controls. I avoided stops in the big towns. We either slept in the ambulance or under the stars, or sometimes we were put up by country priests, who we felt did not present any risk of betrayal. The weather was beautiful, and we made good progress as far as Budapest.

I had known Budapest before the war, a lovely town extending along the banks of the Danube. It had suffered greatly. All the bridges had been damaged, leaving the river to flow between the remaining pillars. We crossed on makeshift bridges over the legendary waters, which were disappointingly grey and melancholy. On sections of bare walls that were still standing, graffiti in huge letters caught the eye, which read 'Long live Rákosi'. Rákosi, the Secretary-General of the Hungarian Communist Party, was the new leader of the country, imposed on the people by the Russians. Despite his loyal obedience to Stalin, he was still sacrificed in cold blood during a purge a few years later.[14] In Budapest, we spent the night at a French Mission based at a religious seminary. The persecution of Catholics had not yet gained momentum.

The following morning, we set off in an easterly direction towards the plain of Hungary, covered as far as the eye could see with cornfields, a brilliantly shimmering mass of yellow in the intense August sunlight. The monotonous road went from bad to worse. A plume of dust followed our vehicle. From time to time, we passed the odd military vehicle, but there was practically no civilian traffic, apart from carts pulled by half-starved horses or by oxen. The sparsely scattered villages we drove through were all deserted. I suppose that when they heard a motorised vehicle, the terrorised locals hid indoors. We reached Sighet, a curious little town with narrow medieval streets, where the population was half Romanian and half Hungarian. Then, soon after turning northwards, we were able to make out the violet contours of the Carpathian Mountains in the distance. As we neared the mountain range, the road surface deteriorated with appallingly deep craters. We were forced to raid our stock of inner tubes.

We were now entering what must have been the most backward part of Europe – sub-Carpathian Russia, and it was just here that the most dreaded thing happened: we broke down. Our overloaded ambulance was not built for such bumpy roads; an axle had broken. Roger, normally so courageous, was beside himself. He sat down at the roadside and wept. "Lieutenant, do you think we will ever see France again?" I forced myself to reassure him, as I was not convinced either. Then I set off for the nearest village, inhabited by Ukrainians. Eventually, I managed to convey what was needed through sign language and some men led me to an old Chevrolet car, which was half buried and largely derelict. Miraculously one of its axles was still intact.

Clearly, this axle was of no use to these people, but equally, they well understood that it was essential for me. For them to let me have it, I had to sacrifice some petrol and food. We worked all through the night with the village blacksmith (who used a pair of bellows as in bygone times) to adapt the axle taken from a Chevrolet car to fit our ambulance, a Dodge. And the three of us continued for most of the next day as well. At last we finished – and hallelujah! It worked!

And so, we set off again on our way. To his surprise, I had stopped asking Roger to put his foot down. For once, I allowed us the time to admire the wild charm of the mountainous scenery. I chose a spot for a picnic. We stopped at another to bathe in the river Tisa. After this, I followed a plan. I calculated that the best time to cross the Russian border would be at nightfall. Just as the sun was setting, we caught sight of a mound blocking the road at the top of a pass. We realised that this was a machine-gun nest guarded by Russians, and that it was also the border. Right beside it was a little cottage.

I got out and walked towards it. As I was hoping, the sentry of this godforsaken post in the mountains was a soldier. He even spoke a little German. I gave him to understand that I was on an official mission entailing the repatriation of French prisoners. I asked him for hospitality and whether my ambulance could be guarded by a member of his staff. I proffered my forged commission order. He took it from me without so much as a glance and signed it. Why would he bother to check it? Didn't I just tell him that I had come from Paris? I would have had to have gone through so many checkpoints coming all that way. Furthermore, could he possibly imagine, this soldier, that anyone would have the nerve to enter the Soviet Union if his papers were not in order? He gave me everything I asked for and went off to make up a bed for me. Roger was to sleep in the ambulance. We spent the rest of the evening pleasantly, chatting, playing dice and drinking a glass of vodka.

At daybreak on the fourth day of the journey, I entered Soviet Russia. From the Carpathians, I descended to the plain of Ukraine without having to undergo any more controls. As we were entering Bukovina from the north, the familiar sight of my birthplace suddenly came into view: Czernowitz! I experienced a moment of intense emotion. Almost simultaneously there followed a feeling of anxiety. We had succeeded in making the outward journey, Vienna to Czernowitz. But our ambulance was very much the worse for wear, and we no longer had a single spare tyre and were running very low on petrol. To undertake the return journey of seven hundred and twenty kilometres would be madness. Very quickly I made up my mind. The decision I made was not out of choice but dictated by the circumstances...

I was just outside Czernowitz. I could have gone straight on to meet my mother. But if I had gone there first, I would have put everything in jeopardy. I ordered Roger to drive the ambulance to the Russian commander and presented myself to the colonel in charge of the city. In my hand was the commission order. I was fully aware that I was risking my liberty and quite possibly my life. I explained to him in German that I was on my way to Odessa but that the state of my vehicle was preventing me from continuing my journey safely. His reaction was just the same as that of the border officer – he accepted my story and the documentation without a second thought.

He then provided me with a jeep and an assistant, and with the ambulance following, we drove on to Sadagora, a small village about fifteen kilometres outside the town (where the Hassidic Jews had settled) currently the site of the administrative centre of the third Russian army. My ambulance was fully serviced, and I was provided with enough petrol for the return journey.

Only then could I give way to the feeling of overwhelming happiness at the prospect of being united with my mother. My feet automatically found the way to the house of my childhood, where my mother was still living. Despite my uniform, despite my wholly improbable presence in Czernowitz, she recognised me immediately. But I had a terrible shock: my mother had always looked very young for her age, so young that everyone used to take her for my older sister. The picture of her I had faithfully kept in my mind had always been that of a young woman. Now, I was looking at an old lady with a deeply lined face and completely white hair. I could instantly see the ordeal of years of war with all their deprivations, restrictions and anxieties engraved on her face. Miraculously, she had escaped the large-scale massacres and deportations of the Jews under the German and Romanian occupations. But my father had died and since the liberation, that is since the inauguration of the Russian regime, two or three rooms in her flat had been requisitioned for Soviet officials, and accommodation was so scarce that she had been forced to share the remaining room with another woman. True enough, she no longer had to fear for her life, but without work, stripped of possessions, she was vegetating rather than living, having had to sell first her furniture, then clothing and any other possessions she could. She had lost all hope of ever seeing her children. Words cannot describe our emotion at seeing each other again. Our joy was immeasurable.

"I have come to collect you," I told her. "I am going to take you back with me, but you must leave all your possessions behind – all the things you treasure and the art books you have collected throughout your life. Don't take any written material, just the minimum of personal effects." It was perhaps a little naïve of me to imagine that if I were arrested at the border, that the guards would believe my story that I was transporting my mother, rather than attempting to smuggle any goods out of Russia.

The ambulance was parked in the courtyard of the house next door. Roger stayed inside it, guarding the precious petrol supply. Time was passing rapidly as my mother and I conversed. So much had happened since our separation. We spent much of the time talking about my father. How I wished I could visit his grave where he had been buried three years previously.[15]

Dawn was breaking on the sixth day of my journey as we set off on the way back. I took the same route as before, hoping that I would have the same luck again. We arrived without any incidents at the machine-gun nest. I made my mother lie down inside the ambulance and we stopped two hundred metres away from the barrier. Then I instructed Roger to drive the ambulance very slowly until I gave him a signal to stop. I went up to the border policeman's cottage, where I met the Russian lieutenant, who gave me a cordial reception. I spoke to him about Russia. A beautiful country but what awful roads! We exchanged visiting cards and I invited him to come and see me in Paris. He countersigned my mission order, which I have carefully preserved as documentary evidence of the episode. I gave Roger a signal from the entrance of the house and very slowly, the ambulance approached the mound. A single gesture from the officer to the sentry and the impossible happened: the barrier was lifted and the ambulance containing my mother passed through the frontier.

By the time we had entered Hungary, my mother must have been quite uncomfortable inside the ambulance. I got her to move into the passenger seat next to the driver. I thought it was going to be plain sailing from now on. But I was wrong. Suddenly, there appeared a detachment of Hungarian military police, who evidently found the presence of a woman in a military vehicle unacceptable. They commanded my mother to get out. But I was not having any of it. I shouted back at them, "You have lost the war and you are not going to lay down the law to a French officer. If you don't watch out, I'll stop the first Russian vehicle that passes and then you'll be sorry."

This worked, so great was their fear of Russians. "You may pass," the Hungarian soldier said. And that was the last incident to occur on our trip. After three more days, without further hitches, my valiant driver deposited us at our destination, the capital of Austria. That was the end of an adventure for which, out of pure loyalty to me, he had chosen to risk his liberty, his happiness and his life.

The first thing I did was to go and see General Ch***. I told him the whole story and reassured him that all had turned out for the best, since he had been worrying a great deal about me. The next day I received a telegram ordering me to return to Paris immediately. This left me only a few hours to make the necessary arrangements for my mother...

As a Soviet citizen she had no papers with her. I eventually managed to take her to Bussières, where I had lived and practised as a doctor and everyone knew me. The mayor created an identity card for her, which enabled me to take her with me to Paris. And that is the story of how I rescued my mother. I am always moved when I remember her last words to me: "I ask myself if I was a good daughter to my mother, but I want you to know that whatever happens, you have been a very good son to me."

13

ADJUSTMENT

When Reinhold was demobilised in 1945, he found himself at a crossroads in his medical career. Later, looking back on his life, he reflected, "My lucky break, even though it is cruel to say it, was thanks to the war, England and anaesthetics." He was burning to put the wealth of experience in anaesthetics he had acquired in England to good use. However, this was not going to be easy.

In France at the end of the war, patients were generally put to sleep before operations by means of ether or chloroform, as had been the practice throughout the previous century. These substances were administered via a simple piece of equipment, the mask of Ombrédanne.[16] During his time in England, Reinhold had become proficient in the use of the modern anaesthetic machine, which was designed as a closed circuit. This was a way of regulating the breathing artificially, via an endotracheal tube delivering modern anaesthetic gases. He knew that this method greatly reduced the mortality and complication rates of operations. Reinhold was the first doctor to present these latest ideas to the French Society of Anaesthesia. He was taken aback to find that the concepts were met with hostility. The president of the society accused Reinhold of sacrilege, pronouncing that 'God has given us breath, and only God has the right to withdraw it'.

Reinhold was offered a post in the *Hôpital Foch*, a military hospital, to join the team of a colonel-surgeon who had worked with him and had been impressed with his results during the war. However, the chief administrator of the hospital refused to provide Reinhold with the equipment he needed, blustering, "We have been using the mask of Ombrédanne, to the great satisfaction of all for the last hundred years.[17] I really don't see the need to change it for costly foreign methods." Reinhold had to resort to buying his own equipment. As he did not own a car, he struggled into the métro with a towel stuffed with instruments and medical products in one hand, and in the other, a very heavy anaesthetic machine. On his back was a rucksack full of explosive and highly combustible oxygen, ether and cyclopropane.

The first occasion Reinhold used his equipment took place prior to a difficult abdominal procedure. Afterwards, the theatre sister disdainfully threw some coins in his direction amounting to two hundred old French francs – about forty pence in today's money. It was the custom to tip the orderly in charge of sedating the patient. On another occasion in the *Hôpital Foch*, Reinhold was asked to anaesthetise a patient who was to undergo a complex urological operation. In accordance with his usual practice, he checked that all his equipment was in order before the surgeon arrived. However, when he came to open the oxygen bottle, he found, to his horror, that both it and the spare one were empty. He quickly realised what had happened: the theatre orderly had stolen his full bottles and replaced them with empties! The young man protested his innocence, but fear got the better of him when Reinhold threatened him with imprisonment. He duly returned the stolen bottles. To add insult to injury, when Reinhold reported the incident to the medical director, the response, no doubt accompanied by a Gallic shrug, was, "Well what do you expect? You have taken his living away from him. And anyway, I don't hold with having a so-called anaesthetic expert in my clinic either." This was the prevailing attitude amongst most surgeons in France, who considered anaesthetists a threat to their prestige.

Although Reinhold was determined to forge a career for himself in anaesthetics, he was finding it difficult to earn enough to support himself, Fa and Annie, who by now had re-joined the couple and was living with them as their daughter. They had to make do with Fa's meagre army salary, and most of their friends advised him to cut his losses and find a lucrative practice to take over as a general practitioner. However, with Fa's encouragement, he persevered in the pursuit of his unvalued vocation. Little by little, his reputation grew, as he worked in the *Hôpital Foch*. He produced many papers for scientific journals about the latest developments in anaesthetics, including the use of the barbiturate, sodium pentothal, in combination with curare.[18] Later, Reinhold led the way in the introduction of the technique of 'controlled hypotension', which enabled surgeons to operate in a virtually bloodless field.

In 1948, now working in the prestigious *Hôpital Cochin*, Reinhold became Professor of Anaesthetics at the Faculty of Medicine in Paris. As he admitted in his autobiography, "It was a great personal success, for I had overcome a big handicap. I was a foreigner, I was Jewish, and I hadn't climbed the conventional medical ladder." Before his death in 1969, he was able to reflect with pride that nearly all the anaesthetists in France were his 'children' or 'grandchildren'.

*

After Martha's perilous escape from Czernowitz, Reinhold managed to obtain permission for her to stay with him, Fa and Annie in Paris. This, naturally, had not been straightforward, and Reinhold had resorted to using his influence to circumvent the bureaucracy. Not long after her arrival, Martha herself underwent surgery on both her feet in the *Hôpital Foch* where Reinhold was working. Martha was one of a few non-military patients there. Finding herself surrounded by wounded and recovering soldiers, she was fascinated, noting down some impressions of the time she spent there as an inpatient. The diary is written with her characteristic compassion and humour.

Martha was deeply impressed by the skill of the surgeons, who 'cut and sewed living flesh like tailors as if it were silk or satin'. She was amazed by the practice of modern anaesthesia, which we now take for granted. It was nothing short of miraculous that a patient could be put to sleep before he could count to three, and on waking had no idea that it was all over, when he had been under the knife for hours. She soon struck up a rapport with her neighbour, who had suffered multiple fractures when she was flung ten metres up in the air, after driving over a mine. After eighteen months of rehabilitation, she was longing to dance again and offered to teach Martha the 'Bongi-bongi'.[19] Martha told her friend that she would have made an odd dance partner with her thickly bandaged feet!

Despite the grotesque appearance of the victims of war – men with severe burns, amputations and other mutilations – Martha described the hospital as an immensely cheerful place, where there was a lot of singing and whistling. Young men in high spirits hopped around on their crutches at speed, relieved to have survived, and the long-term patients made themselves at home by putting up photographs of pin-up girls. The hospital was spotless and well run: the saying went that 'in *Hôpital Foch*, no-one dies.' No doubt this was partly thanks to the liberal use of the relatively new drug, penicillin.

The one major downside was the food. Martha found it ironic that, no matter how many regulations were imposed by the Ministry of Food, the problem was not being addressed. There was simply not enough food, and people got heartily sick of daily noodles, potato purée and mutton. They managed to satisfy their craving for beefsteak *saignant* by procuring their own small electric ovens and asking their relatives to bring in meat for them to cook.

The highlight of Martha's stay in the *Hôpital Foch* was a gala evening, attended by the whole hospital, from distinguished soldiers in full military regalia, to the seriously wounded on stretchers – men without noses, men whose hair had turned white after torture, or in one terrible case, a man with a fully reconstructed face devoid of any expression, with a cigarette wedged permanently in one corner of his mouth. This audience howled with laughter at all the jokes and clapped wildly at the singers and dancers, who brought them the charm and gaiety of Paris.

Martha had arrived in Paris in October 1945. The first thing she saw as she opened her eyes on the first morning, was Edith and Ralph's 'dear, sweet wedding photograph' on her bedside table. She was filled with joy to see Edith looking radiant and happy, commenting that she could see goodness and innocence in Ralph's face. With typical fortitude and optimism, she made a quick recovery from all her ordeals, reflecting how very lucky she had been to have come through the war unscathed. "It is a miracle what has happened to me. After all the dangers, I am healthy and intact and reunited with my dearest children who are building a new life for themselves of which I am a part." Fate had chosen her to be one of the luckiest.

By the end of the war, nearly all Martha's friends and all her surviving relations, fearing Soviet rule after their previous experience in 1940, had succeeded in emigrating from Czernowitz. Martha's brother, Robert, gave up his gentleman's outfitters shop in Bolivia, returning to Vienna to resume practice as a lawyer. Her sister, Lili, left Timişoara, Romania, also to spend the rest of her days in Vienna. Life after the war in Czernowitz was bleak at best and potentially risky. Many men were captured and deported to far-flung parts of the Soviet Union, where they were used as forced labourers, to compensate for the great shortage of manpower, the consequence of massive war casualties. Ukrainians and people from other parts of the Soviet Union settled in Czernowitz (now 'Chernovtsy') largely replacing the Jewish population.

The few survivors from the camps were not welcomed when they returned to Czernowitz. Rosa Roth-Zuckermann's experience was typical. As the only member of her family to have survived the concentration camp, she was met with hostility from the new occupants when she returned to her flat. "It was terrible to be all alone in the place where you had grown up." She felt like a foreigner in her own town.

Martha's rapture on learning that Edith was expecting a baby can hardly be imagined and she indulged herself with happy speculations in her letters to Edith: naturally, the baby would be both highly intelligent and very musical. For some reason she and Edith seemed to assume that the child was to be a girl. The favoured names on the shortlist were Dorothy, after Edith's father, Theodor, and Jane, after Ralph's mother, with Bridget as a second choice.

Martha's letters to Edith are full of the stuff of daily life. She could not resist sharing useful recipes, even though she had put weight back on and was restricting herself to a diet of boiled potatoes. Somehow, despite leaving Czernowitz in such a hurry in Reinhold's ambulance, she had managed to salvage quite a few treasured possessions, such as fine silverware and Romanian hand-embroidered cloth. She was looking forward to presenting them to Edith. As ever, Martha's preoccupation with Edith's clothes was a favourite topic, especially in the light of her forthcoming concert in Bath. "Have you got a suitable concert dress? How is your winter wardrobe? Have you got suspender belts, snow boots, trousers... have you bought a maternity bra yet?"

Martha had not long arrived in Paris before they arranged for Edith to visit her there. She had already sensed that her daughter was not coping well with her new life in London. Whilst she could tease Edith about the mishaps she was experiencing with her new electric oven, she did not underestimate the difficulties she was having in adjusting to all the major changes in her life. With motherly concern, she wrote, "My Ederl, your last letter was so distracted. Was it only external circumstances that were troubling you? Are you still having difficulties with your husband? You have started married life a decade late – and what a decade!" A specific concern was the illness of Ralph's father, Alec, which Reinhold had diagnosed from afar as tuberculosis. Reinhold advised Edith to move out of the flat before the birth, so as not to expose the baby to any risk. Subsequently the fear of TB proved to be a false alarm.

Edith visited her mother in Paris for a few weeks in the winter of 1945, which was a great consolation. Her mother's tender letter to her after she left shows that they felt closer to one another than ever. "We are and always will remain one, won't we. You have promised me to look after yourself and the baby... Make yourself a strong coffee with milk in the morning and hang and dry the sausage in a dry airy place. My darling, I kiss you a thousand times."

*

As he was still serving in the British Army of the Rhine in Berlin, Ralph was only able to visit Edith sporadically for a few days at a time. Although life for him in Berlin was comparatively luxurious, he turned down the opportunity to remain there for longer. Evidently, he had plenty of leisure time, since he was able to take up the piano as he always did when he had the opportunity, and even embarked on singing lessons. Edith must have written to him regularly, and it is a little odd that her letters from this period are missing. It is out of character for Ralph to have lost them. Perhaps he was saddened by them, or perhaps now he was married he felt less need to preserve them. His letters were more light-hearted. Thanking her for a parcel she sent him, he said, "I received the packet which consisted of the following:

1. Chocolate hankies
2. Chocolate oranges
3. Chocolate letters
4. Chocolate drawings
5. Chocolate tea (very tasty, that tea)
6. Chocolate sardines

Yes, you guessed it – the box of cocoa burst!"

The drawings he mentioned were for the comic, *Dandy McQueen* (later known as *The Dandy*), to which he was still contributing as a freelancer, presumably writing the text for the speech bubbles of the cartoon characters.

Whenever Ralph returned to London on leave, he had a lot on his mind. He and Edith were desperate to find a flat of their own to rent, to give them more space and privacy, not least a double bed. This was proving very frustrating because of the scarcity of accommodation in London after the Blitz. He was also preoccupied with material worries and scanned the employment columns, even considering a move to Sydney, Australia. His immediate plan, on his return to London in the summer of 1946, was to take whatever temporary work his cousin, Arthur, the publisher, could offer him, whilst applying for university posts and completing his thesis.

All this stress must have contributed to Ralph's moodiness when he came home on leave. No doubt, he too was struggling to adapt to his new state as a married man and was feeling the weight of responsibility for Edith's happiness and well-being. For it was clear that as the pregnancy progressed, she was feeling worse. Although he was not granted leave in time for the expected date of delivery, he was planning to arrive just a few days after. He was finding it difficult to contain his excitement. "By the 24th April, my brother will already be an uncle and the family will all be reunited for the birth of our child!"

Around two weeks before the baby was due, Edith was admitted to hospital for rest, because she had developed high blood pressure. Knowing that she was feeling lonely and isolated, with few visitors to relieve the monotony, Ralph wrote to her as frequently as he could. He told her that a kind young woman in the Officers' Mess was knitting some socks for the baby, and he was proud to say that he had contributed a few rows. Luckily, it had at least been possible to arrange for Martha to travel from Paris to be present at the birth.

After enduring a difficult pregnancy ending with hospitalisation, things went from bad to worse for Edith. She would look back on the delivery of her son as traumatic. 'He tore me', were the words she used, as if this was the baby's fault. She spent a further eleven days in hospital 'lying in', as was the custom for women after childbirth at that period. Ralph and Edith named the baby John Theodor Alexander. They always said that they chose the name John because it was the nearest boy's name to Jane, but perhaps Ralph, still working on his novel, also had its protagonist in mind, or possibly, he may have named his son after Johnny, his close friend from student days.

The first few days after the birth were a stormy time for Edith, who no doubt felt immensely vulnerable, despite her mother's soothing presence. When he arrived, on the fourth day of his son's life, Ralph must have been profoundly shocked to find Edith in such a depressed state, which was apparently deepening day by day. One great source of anxiety and distress for Edith was John's circumcision. There is no record of when the ritual took place. He could have been taken from the hospital on the eighth day of his life, according to the Jewish custom, or the procedure might have been delayed until he and Edith were allowed home. Whether the circumcision was performed at home or in a synagogue is also not known. What is certain, however, is that Edith was totally opposed to it, and that she was overruled by Ralph's family. Ralph's feelings on the subject are not clear. Although he was always secretive and often ambivalent about his Jewishness, at this time in his life his identity was certainly bound up with Jewish culture at a deep level. During the early years of his married life he would kneel by his bed last thing at night and say his prayers in Hebrew.

As far as the extended family was concerned, this would have been a joyful and important occasion, since John was the first male child in a new generation. Flora, one of Ralph's cousins, who was only fourteen at the time, remembers Edith coming into her bedroom, distraught, and sitting down on her bed in floods of tears. The last thing she wanted was for her son to be recognisable as a Jew in an anti-Semitic world. Coming from a completely non-practising family herself, she probably also had a horror of inflicting pain on the tiny creature.

Shortly before Edith and John were discharged from the hospital, she and Ralph reached a crisis. Edith must have tried to push Ralph away completely at this point. They were both trying to understand their relationship and whether they could survive as a couple. The root of Edith's distress was surely the colossal disappointment she must have experienced after the years of constructing an imaginary future with Ralph. Even the knowledge of his true nature could not have killed the hope that, once finally united as man and wife, his feelings might change. It was only now that the cruel truth penetrated viscerally. However great the love and affinity between them, her feeling for Ralph as a man could never be reciprocated: he would never desire her as a woman.

Ralph wrote to her, pleading for the preservation of their marriage. "For me, it is my last chance, I know very well. If I can't find happiness with you, I am finished. It makes me cry to write these words. I know these are the tears of an egoist. It's not for your sake I beg this grace, it's for mine. Can you refuse me this? I cannot believe you would. But I cannot contemplate living with a stranger, a young stranger, whose only connection was that she had adopted my name, a name which I myself have had for such a short time. Think about it, dear friend. God bless you, whatever you decide to do. You must not expect me to be untrue to myself. I will come to see you on Sunday and be ready to take you back to our home that evening, if I get the expected reply. If not, we will have to discuss our future. With a tender kiss to my little mother."

Ralph received the reply he was hoping for and duly took Edith and John home. On returning to the flat, he immediately set about making Edith's life easier, by engaging a cleaning lady and buying necessities for the home such as items of furniture. Even more importantly, realising how essential Martha's presence was for Edith's mental health, he wrote to the Home Office, arguing the case that she should be given permission to stay for prolonged periods of time.

*

Martha returned to England in May 1946 when John was one month old, and Edith was still suffering with depression. She spent the remaining years of her life alternating her visits to Edith in Britain and Reinhold in Paris every six months. It was a very happy ending to her life and little Johnny was, naturally, the apple of her grandmotherly eye. When in France, she missed him terribly. Writing from Reinhold's garden in St Cloud (a suburb of Paris) on a sunny afternoon, with the family dog and little black cat for company, she said, "When I wake up in the night, my thoughts fly to him (John) and that's what makes life worthwhile." She busied herself knitting for him, following every stage of his development closely, from holding a cup, to his first words and potty training.

While she was in London, Martha kept a brief diary in which she recorded her impressions of England and the English. She discussed the shortcomings of British weather extensively. "This summer in London there were hardly three nice days together, and everyone goes out in the morning with a raincoat over their arm, even if it isn't raining. The commonest words in the weather forecast are 'showers', 'cool' and 'cold.'" She concluded that the English, with their national diseases of rheumatism and gout, can only properly warm up if they go to the continent. She was having to wear her woollen underwear throughout the summer, although she boasted that the corset Edith had handed on to her gave her the figure of a young woman. London was not what she had been expecting at all. Instead of a dark, noisy and filthy metropolis, she found, despite the extensive bomb damage, that it was best described as the largest garden city in Europe. The English were 'in love with Nature' and plants thrived wonderfully well in the cool, damp climate.

Martha found the nation's eating and drinking habits hard to fathom. Ice-cold drinks were not to be found anywhere, beer was served lukewarm in pubs even on hot days, and no-one seemed to drink wine. Curiously, people drank lemonade or even tea in restaurants to accompany fish or meat! Perhaps all this explained the nation's evident passion for ice-cream, which, despite being colourless and tasteless, commanded so many enthusiasts that people queued up for it. Recently there had been a lively debate about the much-loved ice-cream. People blamed the street vendors for being responsible for several cases of typhoid. Ice-cream disappeared from the streets, but within a few days, people were back again, licking anywhere and everywhere.

She had formed rather a rose-tinted view of the English. The authorities were not just polite, but positively friendly and approachable. You could regard the policeman on the beat as a friend who was ready to be at your service to help with any problem. Taxi drivers were never rude, quite unlike their counterparts on the continent, and the English public was 'unbelievably helpful to people they do not know'. Everywhere people could be heard to say, 'Can I help you?' without expecting any thanks. This also would be unheard of in Central Europe.

*

It was not until the summer of 1946, when John was three months old, that Ralph was finally demobilised from the army in Berlin. He kept the menu of the farewell dinner he had attended with his unit:

Brown soup
Salmon on toast
Stewed mutton
Welsh rarebit (a dish he disdained ever after)
Apple cake with cream

This was quite a feast just after the war. Seventeen of his colleagues signed the back of his menu with fond farewell messages, including 'Mary loves Ralph' with an arrow going through two hearts. Ralph also kept his card of thanks, signed by Field Marshal Montgomery of Alamein, Commander in Chief B.A.O.R. 1946, which read:

"I feel I cannot let you leave Rhine Army without a message of thanks and farewell. Together as the 21st army group we carried through one of the most successful campaigns in history and as B.A.O.R. we have laid a firm foundation for the occupation of Germany. It has been our good fortune to be members of this great team. God bless you and God speed."

14

AND SO, THEY LIVED

A nd so, at long last, in July 1946, Ralph returned from Berlin to settle down to married life with Edith. Although he had risen from clerk to major during his career in the army, he always referred to himself self-deprecatingly as a 'pen-pusher'. He felt that his work could not be compared to that of Fa and Reinhold, who were both awarded the *Légion d'Honneur* for their contribution towards the liberation of France with the Free French.

Despite all the anxiety concerning his future career, Ralph was very quickly appointed to a post at Edinburgh University, as lecturer in the department of French. The family settled into a spacious flat in the New Town, where they stayed for six years. This was certainly a step up from their lodgings in Stamford Hill, London, enabling them to buy a fine grand piano for Edith, which became her most prized possession. Edith found work teaching the piano in Dunfermline, whilst also practising repertoire for concerts. Strangely, she always contrived to find work out of town: when she lived in Edinburgh, she worked in Dunfermline, when in Cambridge, she taught in South Kensington in London, and when the family moved to Neuchâtel in Switzerland for a year, she taught in Basel. Maybe this was just coincidence, or possibly, it could have represented a need for independence. Ralph and Edith employed a series of nannies to look after Johnny.

In the winter of 1947, not long after their move to Edinburgh, tragedy struck, when Martha came to stay. Two days before Christmas she went out to the cinema on her own one evening and never came back. They found out that she had collapsed on the street. Martha never regained consciousness and died on Christmas Eve at the age of fifty-nine. The cause of death was probably a sub-arachnoid haemorrhage, as she was known to have high blood pressure and heart problems, and her general health had been described as 'poor' when she had landed at Newhaven. Edith was crushed by grief, which rendered her incapable of normal life for at least six months. By all accounts, she struggled to get up in the morning. It must have been a very difficult time for everyone, especially little Johnny, who was not yet two years old.

Once she emerged from her prolonged mourning, Edith's career in Scotland began to flourish. Ralph took it upon himself to act as Edith's agent, liaising with the people responsible for performance arrangements. Initially, this must have seemed the sensible thing to do, since Edith's English was not yet fluent. Always her passionate advocate, Ralph was determined for her to succeed. On several occasions between 1948 and 1950 she was engaged to broadcast on the Scottish BBC Third Programme, for which she earned a fee of five guineas per session. Sadly, none of these recordings have been preserved. In a letter to the BBC outlining one of the programmes, Ralph wrote proudly, "May I draw your attention to the fact that neither the *Emmanuel Sonatine,* nor the *Roussel Trois Pièces* have been performed or broadcast in Scotland before."

Ralph also gave some thought to Edith's stage presence, perhaps taking over the role of 'wardrobe mistress' from Martha, knowing that Edith tended to be oblivious to such matters. He instructed her, when she went to stay with Fa and Reinhold in Paris, to be sure to visit a couturier who would make up a 'little black velvet bolero' for her. She should also buy herself a small bottle of *Chanel 5* or *Molyneux* perfume, a gold-plated brooch and a pair of clip-on earrings. Nylons, he knew, were 'impossible' at this time. Somehow, I doubt that she complied, as she did not believe in spending money on fripperies. For himself, Ralph ordered a large bottle of *Eau de Cologne*. He also felt the need to cajole Edith into buying more everyday clothes. In another letter, he implored her to give him "the pleasure of going immediately to Greenwich Downes[20] to buy yourself the twinset you need".

Edith went on to perform on many occasions in Edinburgh, Glasgow and Dunfermline. Her repertoire was varied, ranging from well-known works by the great composers, to more esoteric pieces. The programmes were interesting and innovative. Always keen to communicate with the audience, Edith enjoyed giving lecture-recitals, which included thought-provoking and engaging introductions to each piece. Although at this period she specialised in the French Impressionist composers, Debussy and Ravel, the concerts often included both older composers such as Couperin, and the contemporary music of Olivier Messiaen.

She was open to new musical ideas and liked to share her original opinions. When introducing Erik Satie's *Danses de travers* to the Scottish French Society, she explained that in her view, Satie was misunderstood because he was later eclipsed by Debussy. She compared Satie's music, with its obscure instructions, such as 'flat' and 'white' and its absence of time signatures or dynamics, to modern poetry, where there are no capital letters or punctuation marks, concluding that 'Satie opened the way to Debussy who liked him very much and played his music a lot'. Referring to the composer, Paul Dukas, she admitted to the audience that his sonata for piano was regarded as the 'terror of the public and performer alike'. She wanted to reassure them that, although the *Sonatine* by the recently deceased Maurice Emmanuel purported to incorporate Hindu modes, no-one should feel intimidated – there was, in fact, nothing in the least Hindu about it, and the second movement represented some of the most beautiful pages of modern music. As for Albert Roussel, his music 'fled from the emotions like the plague!' Looking through Edith's notes for her lecture-recitals certainly makes one eager to hear the music.

She was very well received in Scotland in the late 1940s and early 1950s, attracting good audiences. In a typical review she was acclaimed as a 'charming speaker as well as a brilliant pianist'. Ralph was at pains to promote Edith as an artist in her own right: when liaising with a Mr Brown, who was organising one of Edith's concerts, Ralph asked him to "please ensure that my wife is not referred to on the programme as 'Mrs' – just Edith Leigh, please."

In 1952, Ralph was appointed as a Fellow of Trinity College Cambridge and as a lecturer at the university. Once again, circumstances forced a separation between him and Edith. She stayed in Edinburgh with Johnny for nearly a year, throughout which Ralph only returned in the vacations. In the meantime, he settled into his new post and looked for a flat for the three of them. Edith tolerated this interruption to family life very badly, feeling completely abandoned. It was stressful for them both, even though Ralph wrote constantly and affectionately, visiting as frequently as possible. When they met, there was irritability on his side and resentment on hers. She recalled a most distressing episode: when she was saying goodbye to him at the station, she realised that her tears were not of sadness that he was leaving, but rather because she was asking herself if she still loved him.

Ralph did his best to try to soothe her, writing from Cambridge, "My dearest, do not think that this separation is more painful for you than it is for me. I am missing you already... you and Jo-Jo are the only people that count for me..."

The celebration of Ralph's election, which was announced in *The Times*, was his introduction to college life, which he later came to take completely for granted during his many years as a member of that community. After the ceremony, which took place in the college chapel, and for which he had to wear a cape, gown, white bow tie and mortar board, there was a feast in honour of all the new Fellows, and a reception in the Master's Lodge. Years later, he used to complain that 'not enough is as good as a feast' but on this occasion he was very impressed with the heavy, ancient, silverware, the four vintage wines (including champagne from 1928) and the liqueurs that followed the meal. The talking and drinking only ended at 1.30 in the morning, by which time, he declared, he felt 'so tired that he could hardly hold his pen' and that 'he was too old for such debauchery!' He was now thirty-seven.

Ralph was under immense strain during his first year at Cambridge, having to prepare thirty-two lectures to conform to a relentless timetable and carry out all his duties to the undergraduates whilst attempting to continue with his research. Frequently the pressure led him to work all through the night and life felt 'like a whirlwind'. Although, as he proudly told Edith, his rooms were just off the magnificent Great Court of the college, dating back to 1546, conditions in Trinity at that time were something of a disappointment. There was no running water and no heating, and the furnishing in his rooms was 'hideous'. To reach the 'very rudimentary' bathrooms you had to go downstairs along a corridor and then up a further flight of stairs. Worst of all, if you wanted a bath you had to 'get undressed in your room and go out into the cold or rain in your dressing gown and slippers and umbrella'. He told Edith that her vision of him living like an aristocrat, who would find it difficult to readjust to normal life at home, was very wide of the mark.

A further source of stress and anxiety for Ralph was his father's declining health. With great solicitude, he and Bernie accompanied the elderly man to Nice, where they had arranged for him to stay for the winter of 1952, in the hope that the warmer climate and the sea air might help his 'bronchial asthma'. Ralph was annoyed with Edith for packing his woollen bathing trunks which he found to be full of moth holes 'in crucial places' when he was hoping to go to the beach.

The following February, Ralph received a telephone call from the authorities in Nice, demanding that Alec be repatriated. He had collapsed in the street and was seriously ill. Ralph immediately set off again for Nice with only £5 in his pocket, travelling via Paris so that he could borrow some money from Reinhold and Fa. When he arrived at Nice, he found to his horror that his father was moribund. Already looking like a cadaver, he recognised his son but could barely speak. The logistical complexity of arrangements Ralph was obliged to make to enable Alec to be flown home took up fourteen pages of description in a letter to Edith. Alec died a few days after he was admitted to a London hospital, leaving Ralph shaken and saddened, reflecting on what a hard life his father had lived, with so little joy.

Edith, Ralph and Johnny, now aged seven, moved into 32A Trinity Street, Cambridge in July 1953, when Edith was at a very early stage of her pregnancy with me. There was a great commotion when her grand piano was winched into the flat, causing the traffic to grind to a halt in the centre of town. Ralph had made every effort to find professional openings for teaching and opportunities for recitals for Edith, thinking that the best bet would be to try to arrange concerts in the women's colleges, such as Girton or Newnham.

Perhaps Edith had moderated her desire to forge a career for herself as a concert pianist in Britain, since she and Ralph had agreed that they would try for a second child. She did, however, give a recital at Trinity College when she was three months pregnant. Giving birth for the second time was quick and easy – so quick that she was rushed just in time to hospital in a taxi after her waters had burst whilst she was queuing at Sainsbury's in Sidney Street. In contrast to all the conflict and anguish over the issue of John's circumcision, I was baptised in Trinity College Chapel when I was three months old and welcomed into the Church of England, although my upbringing as a Christian never went any further than that. They named me Martha, after Edith's beloved mother.

Sometime during the late 1950s, Edith gave a public recital in Cambridge, receiving a glowing, if patronising, review in *The Cambridge Daily News,* the tone of which, while unexceptional for those times, would smack offensively of sexism today. Entitled 'Motherhood and Music', it started off with the following: "Mrs Edith Leigh combines the preoccupations of marriage, motherhood and music with an enthusiasm which makes one wonder how she can find time for it all. The wife of a lecturer in French, who is also a Fellow of Trinity, the mother of two young children and a specialist in the interpretation of French post-romantic music, she brought something of the qualities of all three to the platform." Her musicality is briefly alluded to with the comment, "her manner at the keyboard was that of the virtuoso she undoubtedly is" before the reviewer returns to further stereotypical assumptions. "The deprecatory gesture of refusing a second encore was surely that of a comfortable woman who mustn't stay too long because she has to get back to her home and family. It is to be hoped she will not allow her family to claim too much of her time for her to play to us again".

Edith's passion for playing went hand in hand with her intellectual curiosity as a musicologist. She became interested in the early keyboard music of the *Fitzwilliam Virginal Book*, which she researched from the original manuscript in the Fitzwilliam Museum in Cambridge. Having played works by William Byrd, John Bull and Giles Farnaby in that collection, she decided to explore music by William Croft, Jeremiah Clarke and John Blow, which she later performed at Trinity College. She also added to her repertoire some works by James Nares which she had transcribed from the originals. Equally, she maintained her interest in contemporary music, and was always keen to play new works by new composers she had met, some of which were written for her. Edith always suffered badly from pre-concert nerves, even when she played at home to an invited audience. On these occasions, she could not bear for Ralph to be in the same room when she was performing, so he made do with listening whilst sitting on the stairs. Afterwards she would torture herself with self-criticism.

The image constructed of Edith by the reviewer of *The Cambridge Daily News* as a woman preoccupied with motherhood was inaccurate. She was certainly a very loving mother, but she did not allow anything to come between her and her music. Even when nearing the end of her life and on twice-weekly dialysis, she was preparing for a recital on the days between treatments. Throughout our childhood, she delegated the care of my brother and myself to nannies and au pairs, and her anxiety to find someone to look after us throughout the holidays so that she could practise, transmitted itself to me at an early age. She would rather have her hands on the keyboard than be a 'hands-on' mother. While we rarely did anything just for fun with our mother, this could not be said of our father, but Ralph also encouraged Edith and both of us children to make time for her piano. 'Being good' meant not disturbing her when she was practising. He was proud of her achievements and liked to play recordings she had made of herself to friends in his rooms at Trinity. Most of Edith's performances during the 1960s took place in Switzerland, where she was able to take advantage of the many contacts she had made during the war. Her lecture-recitals of British music, incorporating as many as twenty composers, proved very popular in Biel, Basel, Berne and Neuchâtel.

There were several possible explanations for the dwindling of Edith's engagements in Britain. Firstly, Edith was shy and modest by nature, and lacked the personality required of a diva. Perhaps there was a grain of truth in the description of Edith in the review of *The Cambridge Daily News*, as having a manner which did her no favours in the advancement of her career: "…that friendly little nod to the audience at the end of each piece, that bow she made as she left the platform as if joking to a drawing room of friends" which "made a delightful impression on an audience long enough used to the vagaries of temperament to appreciate it". Ralph may have been too preoccupied at this busy and stressful stage of his own career to take as much control as her 'agent' as previously. Although, by now, Edith had perfected her English which had replaced French as the language spoken at home, she still felt, and would always feel, a foreigner and outsider, even in this, the most congenial of her adopted countries.

*

As for Ralph, he was to devote the remainder of his life to the all-consuming and monumental task of editing the *Complete Correspondence of Jean-Jacques Rousseau*. His research often took him abroad, mostly to the National Library in Paris and the archives in Neuchâtel, Switzerland, but he also went to Germany, Sweden and North America. Sometimes he must have felt like a detective as he tracked Rousseau down in obscure country places. Once, as a family we drove all day (in Uncle Bernie's half-timbered Morris Traveller) in search of a castle where Rousseau was supposed to have stayed, only to find a pile of stones.

The first of the forty-nine volumes of *The Rousseau Correspondence* was only published in 1965, when Ralph was fifty. Each volume, as well as consisting of letters Rousseau received and sent, also included any correspondence *about* Rousseau, all of which Ralph annotated assiduously in his impeccable French. This had not been attempted in anything like such detail before, and Ralph's reputation as a scholar grew with the appearance of each volume.

In his obituary of Ralph, Robert Wokler, a distinguished Rousseau scholar in his own right, went to the trouble of presenting some astonishing statistics about *The Complete Correspondence of Jean-Jacques Rousseau*: he had worked out that in the forty-six volumes of the magnum opus that had been published in twenty-three years, there were about three million words of explanatory notes, twenty thousand pages and more than fifteen thousand manuscripts. A further three volumes comprising the bibliography and index of the work, which Wokler and others completed, were published posthumously, to bring the total number of volumes to forty-nine. Meanwhile, Ralph had also continued to add to his valuable collection of eighteenth-century books, which eventually formed the largest collection by or about Jean-Jacques Rousseau outside Geneva.

Clearly, the masculine ambiance of Trinity suited Ralph, allowing him the opportunity of cultivating close friendships. He took pleasure in sharpening his wit against the whetstone of other brilliant minds. As Robert Wokler put it, "His was the Trinity face that launched a thousand quips." The High Table at Trinity brought Ralph into contact with the rich, the famous and the influential. In 1969, he tutored Prince Charles and, as

'Father of the College' or Praelector, also presented him for his degree in 1970.

Edith was, to all intents and purposes, excluded from life at Trinity. In 1952, after much debate, it was agreed that wives of Fellows could be invited to feasts at the High Table on special occasions. Evening dress was compulsory. It was to take a further generation before the College agreed to tolerate the presence of women as members. Many Fellows held the opinion that allowing women to dine at the High Table was a slippery slope, fearing that the conversation would descend to the discussion of washing machines and other domestic topics. To his credit, Ralph could not be accused of sexism. The first woman elected as a Fellow was Marian Jeanneret (née Hobson), whom he had supervised when she was working on her doctorate and had encouraged to stand. As a member of a minority himself, Ralph recognised and opposed the oppression of women.

Of course, the time Ralph spent at Trinity suited Edith, to the extent that it enabled her to immerse herself in her music. Their marriage was founded on a profound respect for their separate vocations, but they also needed each other. Edith tried to ensure that the household ran smoothly, so that Ralph need not be distracted from his work. When performing, she was always anxious not to disgrace her 'great husband'. Whenever Ralph was away, Edith always 'counted the days, no, the hours', until his return. For his part, he always missed her, writing frequently and in detail about his daily life when abroad. The most basic summary of their relationship would be to say that she gave him the unconditional love he had lacked from his mother, and that this was what he needed. They shared the kind of intimacy that included teasing and she enjoyed his humour, adopting his use of Spoonerisms such as the 'Please Chatter' (cheese platter) which was to be offered at a dinner party. There was also much affection between them, as well as outbursts of temper on his side and mollification on hers. Edith had developed a loving tolerance of anything her 'Ralphie' said or did, even when he ran her down, which, sadly, was all too often. Sometimes she could make fun of him too: she wrote to me asking, "Do you know how many fluid ounces there are in a pint of liquid? Your learned father did not know, and I was at a loss to know how much gelatine to add to the tomato juice." The truth was that they were both hopelessly impractical.

Were they happy? I think for Edith the answer was 'yes'. The twenty-seven years of marriage to Ralph had given her security, stability and fulfilment. The hedge of Queen Elizabeth roses in the front garden of the house at Porson Road symbolised for her the haven she had longed for during the war years, and her love for Ralph only deepened with time. She found everlasting inspiration and joy in her world of music, regardless of any disappointment she might have felt in her career, and, despite the vehement views she had once held against motherhood, she was devoted to her children.

What about Ralph? Was he happy? Needless to say, the answer to this question is more complex. Although I do not believe that Ralph was unfaithful to Edith during their marriage, he was certainly attracted to several men, and in some cases formed deep attachments, which caused him unhappiness. This dissatisfaction, I am sure, was one reason why he frequently erupted in irrational outbursts and behaved badly at home. Ralph sought release from tension and unhappiness by writing throughout his life, preserving many poems he had written from the age of fifteen to his seventies. He also left short stories, diaries, collections of aphorisms and a play (about life in a slum), not to mention his novel. In one of his diaries he stated, "I can't stand being alone. I must complain, if only to a sheet of paper." He 'feared isolation as primitive man feared the night'. Much of his writing makes rather depressing reading; already, at the age of nineteen, he wrote, "Oh God, why give us feet if we must crawl?" The predominant themes that preoccupied Ralph from an early age were the futility of life, unrequited love and death.

His novel, *The Onlooker(s)*, which had served as an important outlet for him during his twenties, became more of a burden to him. Writing in 1941, he said: "Initially it was to spring directly from the heart, to convey to an astonished and perhaps disgusted world all my bitterness and anguish, all the unbearable suffering of my passionate yet frustrated adolescence and all the misery of my sunless childhood... Now the deadlock is this – I must write my novel to be free of it..."

It was only well after he got married that Ralph managed to finish the first draft of his novel. Afterwards he did not return to it to edit or polish it further. He adopted the course of his protagonist, John, who at the conclusion of the novel, consciously chooses to suppress his real desires so that he can "...keep sweet. The only way I can do it is to become normal". The price for this would be to forgo complete fulfilment in a relationship with another man. He would "remain an onlooker, but an onlooker sees *most* of the game". Interestingly, Ralph met E. M. Forster in 1961 over lunch with some mutual friends. He found the elderly Forster 'quiet, but still very pleasant'. Forster's novel, *Maurice*, which he completed in 1914, was first published in 1971, shortly after his death. The main character, like Ralph, studied at Trinity College and struggled with the same predicament. Ralph bought a first edition of *Maurice*. The book is dedicated 'To a happier year'.

Judging from Ralph's outpourings, anyone would think he was deeply unhappy most of the time. On the contrary, he was blessed with true *joie de vivre*. This side of his character delighted in many things, and he was happiest sharing moments of rapture with others, such as uncovering delicious, bright red wild strawberries from under their delicate, feathery foliage on a warm summer's day, stroking and admiring the silkiness of a cat's ear, savouring a good wine, letting go whilst listening to a favourite piece of music, or even enjoying a perfect cup of tea. He was perhaps so used to melancholia that he did not always recognise happiness when it was there.

He did, however, struggle with guilt, which grew stronger during Edith's illness and premature death. Edith, like her brother, Reinhold, had polycystic kidney disease. Reinhold was sixty-one when he died and Edith only fifty-eight. The illness first manifested when she was fifty years old, on one of the two family holidays we had, casting a shadow over family life for several years. A few weeks after Edith's death, Ralph wrote:

"We said
For richer or poorer
And it was mostly for poorer.
For better or worse
And things got better and worse.
In sickness and in health
And it was often in sickness.
But still we didn't think that one day death
would hold us to that bargain.
It is too true an evil
And what's to come of all this empty time
The time of absence
Aching for what it lacks?
Absence like silence
Lies like a canker
At the heart of life
devouring everything."

Ralph fell into a prolonged state of depression after Edith's death, constantly blaming himself for not being good enough to her. At this point in his career, he began to be showered with accolades as his work gained recognition. In 1973, he was made Professor of French at Cambridge University, having turned down an offer from Oxford, and visiting Professor at the Sorbonne. Many more honours were bestowed on him besides. Edith's pride in her husband would have known no bounds if she had been with him to collect his C.B.E. from Buckingham Palace in 1977 (although, secretly, he was hoping for a knighthood). In 1979, he received the *Légion d'honneur* from the French government.

Gradually, after several years of mourning, he was able to take control over his life. He sold the family house in Porson Road, and moved into King's Hostel, the oldest part of Trinity College. Situated next to the Chapel and above the lovely bowling green overlooking the River Cam, this was probably the most superb accommodation available. The family cat, Tigger No 3, whom Ralph took to live with him in Trinity, became something of a celebrity, attracting many tourists all eager to photograph him when they encountered him in Great Court.[21] Ralph certainly found peace and contentment in his final home, although, tongue in cheek, he complained that moving a few steps across Great Court to his new rooms, he was now too far away from the shops. As Kit Wright wrote in his poem to celebrate Ralph's seventieth birthday:

"And still the truth remains

That everywhere man is in chains [22]

Except perhaps in King's Hostel"

Ralph succeeded in loosening his chains in the last few years of his life. He was able to form a sexual relationship with another man without the fear of breaking the law, thanks to the 1967 Act of Parliament, which decriminalised homosexual acts between two men over the age of twenty-one. He had reached his late sixties before he finally felt he could express his true self.

EPILOGUE

It was only when I was in my thirties, after I had finished studying and had settled down, that I felt the urge to investigate my origins. I found I was driven to discover as much as I could of my parents' story, and to make sense of the half-truths and inconsistencies I had grown up with. My quest took me to many places of significance to my family. Unconsciously it was also a force that shaped the direction of my life.

One of the places I visited with my husband, Huw, was Bussières, the small town not far from Lyon, where my Uncle Reinhold, Aunt Fa, my mother and my cousin, Annie, had lived before the war until they all escaped from the Nazis in 1942–3. Some older members of the community still remembered Reinhold and Fa. On our way to their house, which was still standing, we bumped into two people who shared memories of Fa, one of whom recalled that she had delivered her sister. Above the front door of the Kerns' house was a plaque inscribed with Reinhold's name, together with the dates he had practised in Bussières, also stating that he had pioneered modern anaesthesia in France. In the town centre, an information board displayed his photograph and a paragraph about his achievements. He had been a member of the team working at the *Hôpital Cochin* that had operated successfully on President de Gaulle's prostate gland in 1964. The mayor gave us a very friendly welcome in the Town Hall, a handsome building which had once belonged to one of the twelve silk weaving companies of the town. He told us that there was a plan to name one of the streets after Reinhold.

In 2001, over a decade after the fall of the Soviet Union, we discovered that it was possible to visit Czernowitz, the home town of my mother's family, now part of Western Ukraine and renamed 'Chernivtsi'. We had seen a film about Czernowitz in London called *Herr Zwilling und Frau Zuckermann*, a documentary by the German director Volker Koepp, about two Jewish people who lived in the town. As I watched the film, I realised that it was quite likely that Frau Zuckermann would have known my grandmother as she was so elderly. After it had finished, Herr Koepp, who was present, gave me Frau Zuckermann's address. In due course, I received a reply to my letter from her friend and carer, Nadja, confirming that Frau Zuckermann did indeed remember my grandmother and other members of the family. She warmly invited me to Chernivtsi.

At that time, Chernivtsi received very few visitors, and the only practical way to get there was with a group tour overland. We went with a German organisation called *Stattreisen*, departing from Berlin. My heart pounded with excitement as we boarded a Polish night train, to what had always seemed to me a mythical destination. Leaving Berlin in the evening, we entered the plains of Poland all shrouded in mist as night was falling. On waking, early the next morning, there were still some hours to go before leaving the flat and foggy Polish countryside behind. Eventually, after changing from the train to a bus, we reached the Ukrainian border at Przemyśl, where our passports were scrutinised three times in the space of about two hours.

As soon as we entered Ukraine, it felt as though we had been transported into the past. There were still many horse-drawn carts to be seen on the pot-holed roads, often with a foal trotting alongside its mother, and there was little sign of any mechanisation, as we passed fields with heaps of pumpkins glowing in the autumn sunshine and solitary elderly men wielding scythes. Rural life was continuing in a timeless fashion: geese strayed in the small plots in front of wooden houses, each with its own well, and cows blocked the road. In the distance, we caught a mirage-like view of the Soviet tower blocks of Lviv (formerly Lwów, when it belonged to Poland, and before that, Lemburg, when it belonged to Austria). It was pitch dark by the time we reached the town of Ivano-Frankivsk (formerly Stanlisławów), rather a spooky experience, because although the pavements were thronging with night life there was no street lighting whatsoever. We arrived in Czernowitz exactly twenty-four hours after leaving Berlin.

We met Nadja on the first evening, when she greeted us with a bunch of red roses in the dark foyer of our hotel, a sinister Soviet building, where the doors and lifts were guarded by elderly men who were probably armed under their military fatigues. Hotel Cheremosh was the best in town at the time, boasting intermittent warm water and a gloomy basement restaurant.

The visit to Frau Zuckermann was an unforgettable experience. At ninety-two years of age, she was remarkably energetic. She must have had exceptional resilience, both physical and psychological, to have survived her multiple bereavements and the unimaginably appalling conditions of the concentration camp in Transnistria. A typical Czernowitzer of her generation, she was fluent in six languages: German, Yiddish, French, Ukrainian, Romanian and English. Following the film, she had become quite a celebrity, and whilst we were with her, her red phone, which was in the shape of a car, rang constantly, making its headlights flash. We sat at a table laden with biscuits and sweets in her small flat, crammed with books about Czernowitz, poetry and literature, whilst she talked animatedly about my family and her memories of the war. From time to time, she broke off to say, "Well, that's enough about me, what about *you*?" and off she went again, before there was time to draw breath. Frau Zuckermann volunteered that she knew where we could find my grandfather's grave, actually very near to where she had planned to be buried herself. She drew a shaky sketch on the back of an envelope for our reference.

Once Huw and I arrived at the Jewish cemetery, we set off in search of Theodor Kern's grave, walking up and down and round and round in vain. Just as we were about to give up, we chanced upon a guide who was showing some French people around. We gave him the dates of birth and death of my grandfather, and he obligingly went to check the position of his grave in the archives. Sure enough, after a few minutes he came bounding back and led us to it. It was hardly surprising that we had overlooked it. The gravestone was small, modest and completely overgrown. Finding it was a very happy moment for us, despite having to crouch on stinging nettles to have our photograph taken. The grave had not been visited since 1945, the year when Uncle Reinhold made his perilous journey to rescue my grandmother. It was even more poignant for me, when I considered that my mother had never seen it.

The Germans who made up most of our group were all interesting and kindly people. As I was the only member of the party who had come on the trip to find my roots, we speculated as to what their reasons had been for choosing to travel to this part of eastern Europe. We suspected that several of them wanted to understand more about their fathers' activities in the war, and that they had come in a spirit of atonement. There was a lot of interest in the various cemeteries we visited and the sites commemorating massacres of Jews, as if some of them were trying to come to terms with a burden of guilt. Their involvement in my progress, and delight at my success in finding traces of my family, were very moving. I wondered what my mother would have made of this rapprochement between German and Jew.

Indeed, the quest for my roots was altogether very successful: Herrengasse, or Jancu Flondor Street, as my grandparents' address was called in their day, was now renamed 'Olga Koblyanska' Street, after a famous Ukrainian poet. Number 47 was still standing, but we were taken aback to find that the whole building had been converted into a public library: the Polish Library from which my grandmother used to borrow six books at a time when it stood opposite her building, had moved across the road in 1947. We were greeted by its Ukrainian director who, revealing a mouthful of steel teeth in her friendly smile, kindly allowed us to wander all over the building. It was in vain that we scoured the second floor for clues that my family had lived there, but were nevertheless confident that this was the case, as my grandmother often mentioned enjoying the afternoon sun on her balcony and this was the only room that fitted her description. It also contained a stove which featured in her letters and is unlikely to have changed.

Perhaps the most precious of the tangible links we still have with Czernowitz is Martha Kern's wedding ring, which she bequeathed to Aunt Fa, who in turn left it to me when she died. I gave it to Huw on our wedding day. Engraved on its inner surface is the name, Martha, with the dates of her wedding, 6th December 1906 and ours, 30th May 1992. We also share Martha Kern's personal collection of recipes with my cousin, Annie,[23] who can claim the memory of inhaling the aromas from my grandmother's kitchen as she watched her making stuffed cabbages (*halushken*), smoked herring with onion, or cucumber in the Russian style. The dog-eared, food-stained recipe book bears stamps in Cyrillic script at the beginning and the end from a Soviet censor, who must have inspected my grandmother's library. It was such a precious possession that Martha was unable to part with it on leaving Czernowitz. Despite Reinhold's injunction not to take any books or written material of any kind, she hid it under her coat throughout the journey.

In her autobiography, Annie describes how it was not until she had reached her mid-sixties, after many years of practising as a psychoanalyst, that she allowed herself to think about the devastating loss of both her parents in Auschwitz. Eventually, she forced herself to revisit the flat from which her parents had been evicted by the Nazis in 1941. On an impulse, she rang the doorbell and asked the woman who came to the door if she could have a quick look round as she had once lived there. Before she could catch so much as a glimpse of the interior, the woman slammed the door in her face. Annie assumed that she must have been related to the family that took up residence after her parents had left. At the time of writing, Annie, the only child of murdered parents, at ninety years of age is the happy matriarch of an enormous family. Her greatest joy is to bring everyone together at Christmas, including ever-increasing numbers of great-grandchildren.

My mother's silence about the holocaust was broken at the point of her death. Her last words, delivered in the mother tongue she had ceased to use for decades, were *'Ich bin nicht Schuld'* ('It was not my fault'). The guilt and terror which tormented her had been violently repressed, only to be released from her unconscious mind during sleep, when nightmares caused her to let out that haunting strangled scream, translating itself into my childhood fears; fears that the doors did not lock properly and that a stranger would get in and take me away. The 'white lies' concerning religion, that my mother thought necessary to protect her children from the evils of the world so that we would have a 'happy childhood', meant that I grew up without knowing who I really was. Although my two closest friends at school were Jewish, I never considered myself as one of their number. Later, when I was in my thirties, the need to understand what had happened took me to holocaust museums all over Europe.

When I was at university in my early twenties, studying English Literature with French and German, I had a 'road to Damascus experience' shortly before I sat my finals. Without knowing why, I felt an overwhelming imperative to change the direction of my life completely, and train as a doctor. It was only later that I understood the reasons for this: my mother had always wanted me to become a doctor, like her adored brother, Reinhold. My desire to make sense of her early death, which had occurred when I had just turned eighteen, together with a need for reparation, were too forceful for me to resist.

It is not altogether surprising that I was drawn to work in the East End, very near to where my father grew up; the place he had made such strenuous efforts to leave drew me towards itself like a magnet. Whilst he wanted to forget what he considered to be a 'dark, backward and abysm of time', I wanted to understand where he had come from. The desire to work as a GP in an under-privileged area (as it was when I first qualified) may also have come from a need to make good Ralph's terrible childhood.

It was also no coincidence that Huw and I were married in Hackney Town Hall, as were my parents forty-seven years previously. We now live within walking distance of the flat in Cazenove Road where Ralph lived with his father, Alec, and his brother, Bernie, during the war, and where Bernie continued to live until his death. The flat had become very run down whilst Bernie was living there; the rent was very cheap because the landlord never repaired the leaking roof or fixed the heating. Poor Uncle Bernie had to wash in the public baths because there was no hot water in the flat. He astonished everyone by leaving the vast sum of a quarter of a million pounds, which he had managed to save during his working life, to his son. I will never forget how foolish I felt at his funeral. Since I did not have any experience of the ritual of a traditional Jewish burial, I embarrassed myself by opening the prayer book the wrong way. Feeling like a stranger at Uncle Bernie's funeral was painful, since I knew him so well and loved him dearly.

Soon after we met, I took Huw to see the house of my childhood in Porson Road, many years after it was sold. There it stood, neutral, bland and suburban, dissociated from the Leighs and all their foibles and neuroses. Signs of the past are obscure and indecipherable to the uninitiated: only I could know about the layers of clock golf which lay buried under the lawn.

Inside the house, as I was growing up, dwelt the shadowy figures of my deceased grandmothers, Martha and Jane, all too present in the internal landscapes of my parents' minds. Having explored their letters and writings in the family archive, I now feel as if I have met them. Not long ago, my grandmother Jane, my father's mother, came to me in a dream. As I was leafing through an album of photographs, I paused at one I had not seen before, a lovely portrait of Jane as a young woman (she was of course forever young since she was only thirty-five when she died). To my amazement, Jane looked straight at me, meeting my eyes, and then she slowly turned her head so that she was in profile, casting her eyes downward with a shy smile. It was exciting and so entrancing. I ran to tell my father that I had seen his mother and that she had communicated with me. Ralph's reaction was completely unexpected. He pushed me away, shouting hysterically through tears that he did not want to know. Barging past me, he disappeared. The wound inflicted on Ralph at the age of nine by his mother when she committed suicide ran so deep that it could never heal. As for my other grandmother, Martha, her lively letters, diaries and even her recipe book have made me feel as if I have got to know her well. I feel as though the love she showered on Edith has been transmitted to me.

Edith and Ralph were buried in the same grave in Trumpington Parish Church cemetery, just outside Cambridge, after Christian funerals. Ralph had survived Edith by fifteen years. In 1987 he succumbed to a massive heart attack. Both John and I were present at his hospital bedside during the awful week it took him to die. He was conscious and fighting for life until his heart stopped, which we witnessed as the screen on the monitor went black, recording the event with the utmost callousness. It was 4.20 in the morning of December 22nd, 1987, the darkest part of the longest night following the shortest day of the year. I drove back in a state of numbed automation to Ralph's rooms in Trinity, where I was staying. As I crossed the silent Great Court in pitch darkness, I saw the most magnificent night sky studded with stars and the Milky Way, as if the signals on Ralph's heart monitor had dispersed into infinity. In the enormity of that desolate moment, I knew that my life had changed forever.

The next morning, John told me that Ralph was gay. Ralph had used John as his confidant and leaned on him in his distress. But of course, I knew already, I knew without being told, in the way that one part of one's mind can be aware without articulating it. When I try to understand what Ralph felt about his homosexuality in relation to me, it seems that his great need to be understood was coupled with a fear that I might reject him. Far from holding back on the subject, he would often discuss it, but only in relation to other people. I knew from an early age, for example, that my godfather (whom I do not remember at all) had committed suicide because he was gay. Ralph often skirted round the subject and may have been very close to telling me the truth about himself. When I was eighteen, he gave me an unconventional present, a book called *My Father and Myself*, the autobiography of J.R. Ackerley, in which the author describes his homo-erotic development in graphic detail – an indication of Ralph's desire that I should understand what being a gay man was like. It saddens me now that he could not talk about the situation more openly, even after my mother's death, and that he did not experience the relief and joy of being accepted and loved by his daughter in the full knowledge of who he really was. Nevertheless, in the last analysis, I feel that his stance was probably right. As an adolescent and a young woman, I might have viewed the situation as a betrayal of my mother, which, especially during the years of her illness, would most probably have been unbearably painful for me. It was better for us both to have an unspoken understanding.

My parents are now long dead. Happily, permanent marks of their existence remain which can be revisited and give comfort. Ralph established an annual piano competition in Edith's name which takes place in Trinity College Chapel. In the Ante-Chapel, there is a brass plaque on the wall dedicated to Ralph, with a description of his achievements in Latin, sharing the wall with other plaques commemorating members of the college who are recognised world-wide for their work, such as Tennyson, Vaughan Williams, Rutherford and Wittgenstein. Ralph's collection of eight thousand volumes of eighteenth-century books relating to Rousseau and other contemporary philosophers was eventually accommodated in a dedicated room, 'The Leigh Room', which was opened in 2001 in the Cambridge University Library.

Sadly, there are no recordings of Edith's public performances, but to our delight, John and I managed to salvage some of her practice tapes which she recorded herself in 1971, shortly before she died, by way of preparation for concerts. These tapes, rediscovered more than thirty years after they were recorded, had suffered considerable deterioration, but miraculously, it was possible to digitally remaster enough music to fill a compact disc. To hear Edith playing after so many years was a very powerful experience, especially those pieces we had not heard since childhood, and we felt an eerie chill at the sound, faithfully reproduced, of her dropping her pencil.

Exploring the family archive has shed new light for me on my parents' relationship, and enabled me to understand that, as my father said, 'there are many ways of loving'. I have investigated family secrets, starting with my father's real name, and have discovered what it means to be Jewish. I can place my family story in the context of modern history. Having enjoyed a lifetime of peace and political stability, I concur more than ever with my grandmother, Martha, in her belief in the importance of being a good citizen of Europe, as we re-enter turbulent and increasingly dangerous times.

Writing the memoir has also allowed me to complete, as well as I ever can, the process of mourning for those I loved and lost early in my life. A few years after Ralph's death, a cousin bought a lovely postcard of The Avenue, which runs towards the River Cam and the Wren Library at Trinity College. The photograph was taken in spring, when the ground beneath the tall lime trees is a brightly dancing pattern of thousands of crocuses and daffodils. On close examination of the postcard, a man could be spotted between the trees with his hands folded behind his back. It was Ralph, who just happened to be there. Some years after the discovery of this photograph, I took Huw for a walk down The Avenue on a brilliant, sunny and breezy spring day. If ever he and Ralph could meet, it would be here, approaching from opposite directions.

BIBLIOGRAPHY

Beiner, H. *Quitter Vienne, 1938: la mémoire retrouvée: une psychanalyste raconte.* 2013, Paris, Harmattan.

Kern, E.R. *Mes quatre vies, 1908–1969.* 1971, Paris, Arnette.

Chavagnac, E. *Ernest Kern: pionnier de l'anesthésie-réanimation moderne en France.* 2013, Paris, Éd. Glyphe.

Vinen, R. *The Unfree French: Life Under the Occupation.* 2006, New Haven, Yale University Press.

Moorehead, C. *Village of Secrets: Defying the Nazis in Vichy France.* 2014, London, Chatto and Windus.

Cordon, C. and Kusdat, H. *An der Zeiten Ränder: Czernowitz und die Bukowina.* 2002, Wien, Verlag der Theodor Kramer Gesellschaft.

Fiedler, A., Ranner, G. and Halling, A. *"...und das Herz wird mir schwer dabei.": Czernowitzer Juden erinnern sich.* 2009, Potsdam, Deutsches Kulturforum östliches Europa.

ACKNOWLEDGEMENTS

With thanks to Anthony Rudolf for his interest and encouragement, Emma Storr, Ruth Taylor, Mimi Sanderson and Peter Bavington for critically reading the manuscript, Ingrid Wilson, Angelina Ilert and Timothy Saunders for transcribing my grandmother's writings from Sütterlin to modern German script. I am also grateful to my cousins Annie Anargyros and Flora Shulman for their helpful recollections about the family. Thanks also to Bruno Chavagnac for giving me permission to use his biography of my uncle in this account, and thanks to all the staff at Matador. Most of all, I thank my husband, Huw Saunders, for his tremendous enthusiasm and generous commitment to the project.

NOTES

1 *Rousseau's English Pension*, R. A. Leigh 1971.
2 Moses Tyson Memorial Lecture 1984.
3 The canopy is a piece of cloth supported by four poles under which the bride and groom stand during a Jewish wedding ceremony.
4 Cortot served as a member of the Vichy Council and was appointed High Commissioner for the arts under the Vichy government. He also performed the piece to a Nazi audience.
5 The members of 'Les six' were Poulenc, Honegger, Milhaud, Auric, Durey and Tailleferre.
6 "When there is no alternative, the devil eats flies".
7 "Believe me, my dear Leigh, you are in my best thoughts and have all my friendship".
8 "You do agree, don't you?"
9 A lustrum is a period of five years – a Roman allusion to a ceremonial purification of people performed every five years after the taking of the census.
10 From *A Train in Winter* by Caroline Moorehead.
11 The British attacked the French fleet from the air and sea

at Mers-el Kébir in July 1940, to prevent the Germans from seizing it and gaining advantage from it. This led to the ending of diplomatic relations between Vichy and London.

12 Berchtesgaden was where Hitler built his country home, 'The eagle's nest' where important decisions about Nazi policy were made.

13 Imre Kertész won the Nobel Prize for Literature in 2002.

14 Rákosi was removed as General Secretary of the Party in 1956 and forced to live in the Soviet Union.

15 This is incorrect. Theodor Kern died in June 1943, which was just over two years previously.

16 Ombrédanne (1871–1956) was a French surgeon who invented an anaesthetic inhaler which allowed the patient to inhale chloroform or ether and air.

17 This was inaccurate, as the mask had only been in use for the previous forty years.

18 Curare was originally used by Native South Americans on the tips of their arrows, to paralyse their enemy or prey.

19 A South American dance.

20 Ralph meant Greensmith Downes, the exclusive ladies' outfitters in George Street Edinburgh at that time.

21 There was a rule at Trinity that cats were allowed but not dogs. When the Master, Lord Butler, had a dog it was therefore always referred to as The Master's cat.

22 This is a reference to Jean-Jacques Rousseau's *The Social Contract*, in which he says, "Man is born free and everywhere he is in chains."

23 To be precise, Annie is my first cousin once removed. She was my mother's first cousin and the daughter of my grandmother's sister.